State Parks of Utah

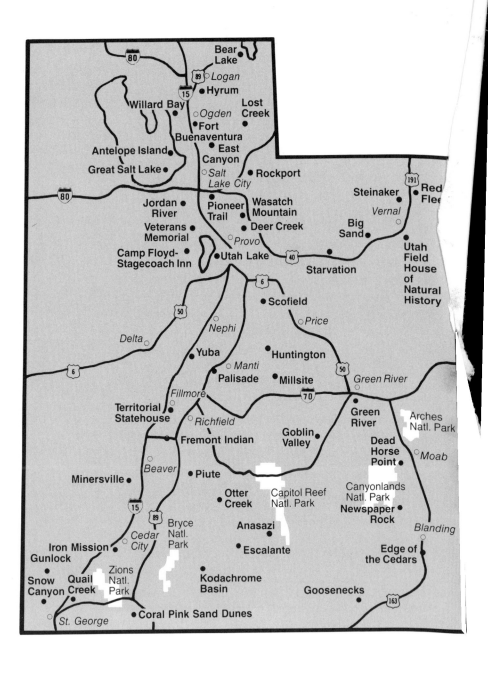

State Parks of Utah

A Guide and History

John V. Young

University of Utah Press
Salt Lake City
1989

Library of Congress Cataloging-in-Publication Data

Young, John V.
    State parks of Utah : a guide and history / by John V. Young.
      p.   cm. — (Bonneville books)
    Bibliography: p.
    ISBN 0-87480-315-2
    1. Parks—Utah—Guide-books. 2. Parks—Utah—History—20th
century. 3. Utah—Description and travel—1981- —Guide-books.
I. Title.
F824.3.Y68   1989
917.9204′33—dc20   89-31524
                                                CIP

Quoted material in Otter Creek State Park description from Revo M.
Young, "Robert D. Young and the Otter Creek Reservoir," *Utah Histori-
cal Quarterly* 53 (Fall 1985), and is used by permission.
The essay "Joshua Trees—Utah's Improbable Lilies" published under title
"In the Desert, Love Blooms between a Moth and a Yucca," by John V.
Young, in *New York Times* Sunday Travel Section, 22 June 1969, copy-
right © 1969 by the New York Times Company; reprinted by permission.
The essay "The Aspen Trees—The Singing and the Gold" published
under title "Magic Becomes Reality When Aspen Leaves Cover the Rockies," by John V. Young, in *New York Times* Sunday Travel Section, 22
September 1968, copyright © 1968 by the New York Times Company;
reprinted by permission.

Front cover photograph courtesy of Utah Travel Council; Frank Jensen,
photographer.

For Emma Lou, constant companion for more than half a century

Contents

viii

Yacht harbor, Saltair, Great Salt Lake State Park (John V. Young)

*Snow Canyon State Park
(John V. Young)*

*Sandwash groundsel, Snow
Canyon State Park (John V.
Young)*

Kodachrome Basin State Park (John V. Young)

Canyonlands from Dead Horse Point State Park (John V. Young)

Dead juniper, Dead Horse Point State Park (John V. Young)

Canyonlands from Dead Horse Point State Park (John V. Young)

*Cascade Springs, Wasatch
Mountain State Park (John
V. Young)*

*Wasatch Mountain State Park
(G. Tenney, State Parks &
Recreation Division)*

Yacht regatta, Deer Creek State Park (John V. Young)

Moonrise, Kodachrome Basin State Park (Tom Shakespeare, State Parks & Recreation Division)

*Goblin Valley State Park
(John V. Young)*

Lichens (John V. Young)

Kodachrome Basin State Park (John V. Young)

*Fremont Indian State Park
(John V. Young)*

*Jordan River State Park (Kay
Boulter, State Parks & Recreation Division)*

Jordan River State Park (State Parks & Recreation Dvision)

Coral Pink Sand Dunes State Park (John V. Young)

Tracks, Coral Pink Sand Dunes State Park (John V. Young)

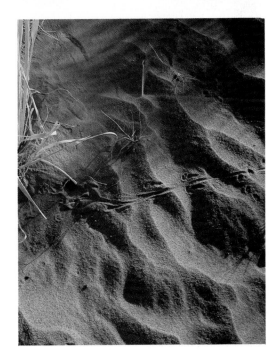

Coral Pink Sand Dunes State Park (John V. Young)

Utah Field House of Natural History State Park (John V. Young)

A Note to the Reader

Whereas the author of a novel, even a historical novel, is free to invent or to modify data to fit the plot, the writer of a nonfiction work enjoys no such liberty. Either the facts as they are presented are indeed facts, or they are not. There is no room for invention or guesswork, and no need for such devices when there is no plot to satisfy. To be sure, as in any human enterprise, there may occur errors—in memory at the source, in perception, in transcription, in note-taking, in simple spelling, in unnoticeable places that not even expert proofreading can detect. For these I apologize.

But well before anything reaches the proofreading stage, the author of a work such as this is wholly dependent upon the good-will, the good nature, and the benevolence of innumerable people, from motel clerks to gas station attendants, from park rangers to strangers met on a trail, whose casual remark can lead to reams of hitherto unsuspected lore.

There are the librarians whose diligent research has produced invaluable biographical backgrounds, old newspaper clippings and magazine articles, photographs of historical characters, referrals to other sources such as regional and local historical societies and compilers of family histories. The Utah State Historical Society in Salt Lake City has been singularly helpful in this respect. Numerous published sources have been credited in this book, but one in particular deserves special mention. It is the 1941 federally sponsored Work Projects Administration *Guide to the State of Utah*, revised and updated in 1982 by Ward J. Roylance, Eugene F. Campbell, and Margaret D. Lester, and copyrighted by the Utah Arts Council, an agency of the Utah Department of Community and Economic Development.

Then there are those special individuals whose contributions rank far above the call of duty. They are Jerry A. Miller, director, and Gordon H. Tenney, former information specialist, Utah Division of Parks and Recreation, and their office staff, as well as all of the people in the state parks who went out of their way to further this project; John VanCott, founding president of the Utah Place Names Society and indefatigable pursuer of little-known information about Utah people and places; Wallace E. Clayton, publisher of the monthly historical edition of the *Tombstone Epitaph*, relentless bloodhound on the trail of historical data and photos, who has filled in many blanks and corrected many errors; Muriel Smith; Mrs. Revo Young; Kathryn MacKay; Bruce Kaliser; Ted Arnow, formerly of the U.S. Geological Survey; Terry Tempest Williams; Frank de Courten, Utah Museum of Natural History; Mark Rosenfeld, Utah Museum of Natural History; Ron Ollis, Utah Division of Water Resources; Tish Poulson, Utah Division of Parks and Recreation; Barry Worth, U.S. Bureau of Reclamation; Joe Anderson, United States Attorney's Office; Delbert Wiems, Department of Biology, University of Utah; Phil Notarianni, Utah State Historical Society; Linda Thatcher, Utah State Historical Society; Curt Sinclear, Red Fleet State Park; Shona Tripp, Yuba Lake State Park; Terry Larsen, Starvation State Park; Dave Stanley, editor; and Norma Mikkelsen, editor, University of Utah Press, without whose patience, perseverance, and hospitality this book could never have been completed.

Introduction

And Some Surprising Park History with a Saying from the Babylonians

One definition of a real Utah old-timer could be a person who can still recall the first attempt to create a state park system in 1925, sixty-four years before this book was written.

A bill to establish a State Board of Park Commissioners passed both houses of the state legislature and was signed into law by Governor George Henry Dern on May 12, 1925. The act called for the governor, the president of the Utah Agricultural College, and two others to serve on the board for a term of four years — without compensation.

The board was given the authority to accept gifts of land or money for state parks and to buy lands deemed "of sufficient natural, historical, or lofty scenic quality to justify such action, if such an appropriation is available." That last "if" was a big one, since no money to buy land was then voted by the legislature. All costs were to be covered by funds allocated by the offices of the governor, the president of the agricultural college, and the president of the state university, assuming they had any money to spare for such an unprecedented enterprise.

Two years later the legislature voted to spend $10,000 to rehabilitate the old Territorial Statehouse at Fillmore, although at the time the building was considered a state monument rather than a park. Even the fate of that appropriation remains a mystery, for the old Statehouse was a deserted shell when the Daughters of the Utah Pioneers rescued it from wrack and ruin in 1930. The building's complete renovation had to wait until the present Division of Parks and Recreation took it over in 1957.

After that futility, the State Board of Park Commissioners seems to have faded away. Various individuals and groups from time to time recommended purchasing places of scenic, geological, or archaeological interest. Among them were Flaming Gorge (now a national recreation area), Capitol Reef (a national monument

Harold B. Fabian, Director, Utah State Parks, 1957–67. Photograph courtesy of Utah Division of Parks and Recreation.

since 1938 and a national park since 1971), and some ice caves near Fillmore. The suggestions went into files, and the state park dream went into limbo for a third of a century.

Then in 1957 the process started all over again, but this time with more success. A new Utah State Parks Commission was authorized by the legislature and appointed by Governor George Dewey Clyde. It first produced a report that foresaw a rosy future for Utah's state-parks-to-be. It proclaimed that "we stand on the threshold of the greatest opportunity for recreation development that will ever be available to the people of Utah. The nation is in the midst of a new era of recreation with thirty-two billion dollars a year spent on recreation in America."

A later report by the commission in 1959 recommended 152 park sites. However, some were repeated in several categories: (1) those for immediate action, (2) those for early action, and (3) potential sites. Of 136 total sites recommended, thirty have subsequently become state parks or state park properties.

During a reorganization of the state government in 1967, the system underwent a major administrative change. A Division of Parks and Recreation was created within the new Department of Natural Resources. The State Parks Commission was dissolved, its foster child off to a flying start. By late 1987 Utah's state park holdings had grown to 94,874 acres of land in forty-eight designated parks. While money is tight, parks are still being upgraded whenever possible and this volume may not reflect all of the recent changes in park facilities.

The Division of Parks and Recreation also has responsibility for enforcement of boating laws on all waters in Utah, which total some 940,000 surface acres. The state, incidentally, has some 840 natural and man-made lakes and reservoirs measuring two surface acres or more, plus 5,400 miles of streams. According to a saying sometimes attributed to the ancient Babylonians, "the gods do not deduct from man's allotted span the hours spent in fishing." If that is true, many of the millions of people who visit Utah's state parks are likely to live a good long time since well over half of the parks offer angling as an attraction. Twenty-one of the parks are on lakes or streams and one, Utah Lake, has been a major fishery off and on since prehistoric times. The native Indian people there were known as the Fish Eaters.

Fishing is not confined to the summer months on many of the lakes. Those at higher altitudes that freeze over in winter attract surprising numbers of fishing fanatics who like to freeze their fingers over holes chopped in the ice. At Bear Lake, lake trout up to thirty-two pounds are claimed as prizes among the fifteen species of fish taken there. The lake also holds an odd little antique whitefish called the Bonneville cisco, which can be caught only in the dead of winter when they swarm near the shoreline to spawn.

Although not all the entrance signs have yet been changed, in 1985 the state legislature changed the status of all the state recreation areas, state beaches, and state historical monuments to state parks, including some that are quite undeveloped and without any public facilities.

In early 1988 the Division of Parks and Recreation decided to drop several small holdings from the list of designated state parks for a fairly obvious reason: they never should have been called parks in the first place. Included in this category were *Danger Cave* and *Bonneville Salt Flats* near Wendover, far out on the western edge of the Great Salt Lake Desert, and *Fort Deseret*, southwest of Delta. *Danger Cave* is an archaeological site originally excavated between 1939 and 1955. Artifacts indicate human occupancy of the cave as far back as about 8,000 B.C. Danger Cave was given its name when a huge boulder fell from the roof during an early excavation, narrowly missing several of the scientists. World land speed records have been set, broken, and rebroken for decades at the *Bonneville Salt Flats*, along Interstate 80 a few miles east of Wendover, where speed demons have been racing various kinds of vehicles since about 1914. The site is administered by the federal Bureau of Land Management, and the only facilities are some restrooms and an observation stand. *Fort Deseret* is a pile of crumbling ruins dating from 1865 near the village of Deseret on State Highway 257 just south of its intersection with U.S. Highway 6 and 50, six miles southwest of Delta. The tiny fort was hastily erected by pioneer Mormon settlers against Indian attacks that never came. The site has no facilities.

From the old Territorial Statehouse to the newest park, Red Fleet, in the northeastern corner of the state, Utah's state parks offer a variety of small wonders. Generally overlooked by the federal government as too small, too regional, or too remote, often bypassed by the casual tourist enticed by the state's better-known national parks, monuments, forests, and recreation areas, these sites offer the visitor a different kind of experience. In these parks are spectacular scenery, vivid examples of Utah history and prehistory, and recreation ranging from fishing and boating to four-wheeling and rockhounding. The state parks have preserved for all time resources that might otherwise have been lost, and expansion of the park system in years to come will ensure that future generations can enjoy these magic places.

Reservations at the parks may be made by telephoning MISTIX Corporation, 1-800-284-2267 from 8:00 A.M. to 5 P.M. Monday through Friday and 8 A.M. to noon on weekends. Unreserved sites are available on a first-come, first-serve basis.

Fees for day-use and camping are charged at many state parks. Additional fees are charged for activities such as skating, golfing, boat mooring, and so on. Fee schedules are available at the parks or from Parks and Recreation, 1636 West North Temple, Salt Lake City, UT 84116-3156; telephone (801) 538-7220.

Calf Creek Falls, 1984. BLM photo by Jerry Sintz.

Anasazi State Park

Open all year   Visitor center/museum
Day-use only   Drinking water
Picnicing   Modern restrooms
Museum; partially excavated Anasazi Indian village; photography.

The paving of scenic State Highway 12, which connects Capitol
Reef and Bryce Canyon national parks, has brought a flood of
new visitors to the once remote village of Boulder and its principal
attraction — Anasazi State Park.

Established in 1960, this little six-acre historic park originally
bore the weightier but more informative name of Anasazi Indian
Village State Historical Monument. It consists of a modern
museum building built in 1970 on the town's main street (which is
also the state highway) and a series of partially excavated, stabilized Indian ruins dating from about A.D. 1075 to 1275.

The park has modern restrooms in the museum building and a
small picnic area but no overnight camping facilities. It is open all
year during daylight hours. A small admission fee is charged.

Long known to archaeologists, the ruins were excavated in
1958-59 by a team from the University of Utah. They uncovered a
total of eighty-seven rooms including living quarters, ceremonial
and burial chambers, and storage bins. When the project ran out
of funds, the site was covered with plastic and dirt to protect it
from weather and vandals.

Reexcavation and stabilization of the ruins were resumed in
1978 and still continue as funding allows. In addition to a full-
scale, six-room replica of a typical Indian dwelling of the period, a
self-guiding trail winds through the exposed ruins for the benefit
of visitors. Excavated artifacts are displayed in the museum.

Of special interest to many visitors is a scale-model diorama
that depicts life in the mud, stone, and timber dwellings that were
accessible only by ladders through the flat roofs. Figurines of a
dozen or more of the inhabitants go about routine chores such as
pottery making, building repairs, carrying water, grinding corn,
and bringing in game.

1

Full-scale replica of a typical Anasazi dwelling.

The inhabitants presumably were members of a great culture that flourished in the Four Corners region of Utah, Colorado, Arizona, and New Mexico from about A.D. 1 to A.D. 1300. They were a diverse and adaptable people generally referred to as the Anasazi, from a Navajo term for "the ancient ones."

As is the case with so many other prehistoric ruins of the Four Corners region, no certain cause is known for the seemingly sudden abandonment of the village, although some possible reasons may have been overcrowding, the exhaustion of natural resources, or invasion by some hostile alien culture. The village may have been burned when it was abandoned.

Because of the village's well-watered location on a branch of the Escalante River, sheltered by high cliffs at an elevation of 6,700 feet above sea level, it is believed that the inhabitants may have enjoyed a more favorable situation than those of many other settlements of the period. They appear to have been able to raise abundant crops of corn, beans, and squash to supplement the nuts, seeds, and berries of the region. Small game, deer, and bighorn sheep were hunted with spears and bows and arrows, and by trapping.

Resettled by Anglo-Americans almost 700 years after it was abandoned by the Anasazi, the tiny town of Boulder is named for the large, dark, volcanic boulders visible on the slopes of nearby Boulder Mountain, the northern end of the vast, nearly unoccupied Aquarius Plateau. Until 1935 the town of Boulder had the distinction of being the last place in the continental United States to have its mail brought in by mule train, which traveled over thirty miles of rough terrain from Escalante.

An enterprising citizen once disassembled a pickup and transported it by mule, piece by piece, to the town where it ran without a state license for eight years. Gasoline at Boulder cost seventy-five cents a gallon then, three times the price outside.

As a Work Projects Administration project during the Great Depression of the 1930s, an auto road of sorts was finally constructed over a heart-stopping, knife-edged ridge called "Hell's Backbone." The road spanned a deep canyon on a one-lane timber bridge, said at the time to be the world's highest. Despite the obvious hazards of the route, it was traversed for years by a school bus without incident. An improved, less dangerous road was eventually built in 1940. Present-day State Route 12 from Bryce Canyon to Boulder winds and twists through spectacular scenery, bordered by cliffs and pinnacles and outcroppings of red and yellow and a dozen other hues of Navajo sandstone, and accented by groves of conifers. The road crosses the Escalante River (last important stream in the continental United States to be explored), where it is a peaceful little creek much of the year. Nearby trails lead to waterfalls, prehistoric ruins, and other attractions in the Bureau of Land Management's Calf Creek Recreation Area.

The section of State Route 12 that connects Boulder to the town of Torrey, just west of Capitol Reef National Park, made an expansive, lake-filled plateau of incomparable majesty and beauty readily accessible to the casual motorist much of the year. Winter travel can be difficult, so inquiry should be made before attempting the trip.

The new highway ascends the northern shoulder of the Aquarius Plateau at an elevation of 9,200 feet amid some of the most awe-inspiring vistas in the nation. The first and perhaps the best description of the area ever published appeared in Clarence Dutton's 1880 *Report on the Geology of the High Plateaus of Utah*. One of the most influential explorer-geologists of his era, Dutton frequently abandoned formal governmental prose in his

The Escalante River enabled the Anasazi to raise abundant crops.

enthusiasm for the scenery he so admired. "The Aquarius," Dutton wrote,

> should be described in blank verse and illustrated upon canvas. The explorer who sits upon the brink of its parapet looking off into the southern and eastern haze, who skirts its lava-cap or clambers up and down its vast ravines, who builds his campfire by the borders of its snow-fed lakes or stretches himself beneath its giant pines and spruces, forgets that he is a geologist and feels himself a poet. . . . We are among forests of rare beauty and luxuriance; the air is moist and cool, the grasses are green and rank, and hosts of wildflowers deck the turf like the hues of a Persian carpet. The forest opens in wide parks and winding avenues, which the fancy can easily people with fays and woodland nymphs. . . . Upon the broad summit there are numerous lakes—not the little morainal pools, but broad sheets of water a mile or two in length, their basins formed by glaciers. . . . It is a sublime panorama. The heart of the inner plateau country is spread before us in a bird's-eye view. It is a maze of cliffs and terraces lined off with stratification, of crumbling buttes, red and white domes, rock platforms gashed with profound canyons, burning plains barren even of sage—all glowing with bright color and flooded with blazing sunlight. . . .

Except for the highway and a few dirt roads wandering off, the scene is much the same today. Another popular road, presently unpaved but usually passable, leaves Boulder and heads across the Waterpocket Fold, intercepting State Route 276 just north of Bullfrog Marina on Lake Powell. There a recently established auto ferry crosses Lake Powell (*see* Goosenecks of the San Juan State Park for more details on this route).

Local inquiry is always advisable on this road, the so-called Burr Trail, which is not for the timid nor for drivers of motor homes or large trailers, nor indeed for anyone in wet or snowy weather. As of 1988, funds for realigning and improving the route had been committed but were being challenged in federal court by environmental organizations wary of the effects of increased traffic.

Flooded entrance booth and gate at mainland end of causeway to Antelope Island State Park.

6

Antelope Island State Park

Temporarily closed; check on access
Camping, 125 units
Group camping
Picnicing
Group pavilion
Modern restrooms,
   wheelchair accessible

Vault toilets
Showers
Sewage disposal
Boating/fishing
Swimming
Concessionaire

Largest island in the Great Salt Lake; salt water bathing; camping; hiking; photography; sightseeing; sunbathing.

Utah's largest state park, all but unknown to many Salt Lake City residents and — as of 1989 — closed to the public, reaches its 26,000 rugged island acres off the Great Salt Lake's eastern shore less than a dozen miles as the seagulls fly from the capitol dome.

But lacking any road or ferry, the island park for the average citizen might as well be on the moon. Without easy access or potable water, the park has been virtually unvisited in recent years, and was finally closed altogether for safety reasons. Its future as a spectacular public playground appears as uncertain as the fluctuating level of the Great Salt Lake itself.

Antelope Island was added to the roster of state parks only recently, although its recorded history dates back to the early 1820s. In 1969 the state purchased some 2,000 acres at the northern tip of the island as the nucleus of an ambitious recreational project that depended on a seven-mile earthen causeway supporting a paved road linking the island with the mainland near the town of Syracuse, just south of Ogden.

For the next several years visitors flocked to the island for picnics, camping, hiking, nature study, and sightseeing. Artesian springs supplied good fresh water, presumably flowing from the Wasatch Mountains on the mainland through deep subterranean strata.

Violent storms on the lake severely damaged the causeway in 1974. Two years later it was rebuilt at a cost of $1.7 million and once more the park attracted more than half a million visitors a

7

year, even though most of the island was still fenced off as private cattle range.

Encouraged by this enthusiastic public response, the state purchased the rest of the island in 1981 and invested more than $2 million in further development. A paved parking lot, picnic shelters, and restrooms were built at Bridger Bay, near the western end of the causeway. Twenty miles of gravel roads and six miles of pavement were constructed to afford access to elevated viewpoints and to other picnic areas on the island.

However, the antic gods that govern the lake had other ideas. The lake kept right on rising, and by 1982 the causeway was under water, along with most of the island's beach frontage and its new facilities, including the artesian wells and springs that had provided water for human consumption. A commercial ferry service ran briefly, but ceased operations after state health officials found the water supply unsafe for human use.

"LAKE SWALLOWS ISLAND PARADISE" trumpeted a headline in the *Los Angeles Times*, an example of the many untruths and half-truths that have circulated widely in recent years. An island paradise it might be — for those who love rugged rock and stark cliffs — but swallowed by the lake it was not. Geologically one of a series of small mountain ranges trending north and south, the island soars to an elevation of nearly 6,600 feet above sea level, about 2,400 feet above the lake. Along the front of the Wasatch Range to the east, wave terraces show clearly how deep was the vast inland sea that geologists call Lake Bonneville during and after the last Ice Age. Still, the terraces are no more than a thousand feet or so above the present lake, and even a return of Lake Bonneville, though it would certainly swallow all the cities and towns in the area, would still be short of covering the island.

Nevertheless, by early 1987 the lake had reached its highest level in modern times, higher by a fraction of an inch than it was in 1872 when it reached nearly 4,212 feet above sea level. Some geologists predicted that with continued wet weather it could rise several more feet and further inundate industrial and residential property on the mainland at a cost of hundreds of millions of dollars.

It was then that the state legislature decided to spend about $60 million to build a giant pumping plant far out in the desert on the western shore of the lake in a desperate attempt to lower the water level. Three huge pumps fueled by natural gas took water from the lake to a low-lying desert area to the west—the so-called "Newfoundland Evaporation Basin," named after a nearby mountain range. The pumping project and two years of drought had, by late 1988, lowered the lake by nearly six feet—so low, in fact, that turning off the pumps until such time as the lake begins to rise again was a real possibility. Previously, local wags had produced posters showing Salt Lake City entirely under water except for the spires of the Mormon Temple, and someone supposedly put a sign on the front lawn of the State Capitol reading "Last One Out, Turn Off the Pumps." Huge expenditures for this project and uncertainty about the lake's movement halted, for the time being, repair and expansion of facilities on Antelope Island and plans to renew public access. Meanwhile, back on the island, a herd of 500 bison still grazed the grasslands, apparently unaffected by all the tumult and shouting except perhaps to notice that there were hardly any pesky humans around to annoy them or to chase them in gas buggies. The big shaggy creatures forage on native grass and herbs, find water at seeps and springs, and seemingly don't mind if the water is a bit on the salty side. They run away like deer when approached by vehicles, but it is quite unwise for anyone to get near them on foot. Their tempers are unpredictable, especially during the rutting season or when small calves are present. For all their shyness, these are dangerous beasts.

First imported as an experiment in 1892 (the herd had previously been an attraction at the Lake Point resort), the bison were supposed to be crossed with domestic cattle to produce a hardy hybrid capable of withstanding the island's sometimes fierce winters. The breeding experiment failed, but the bison survived. Now the herd is kept at its present level by systematic culling. Occasionally some of the animals are rounded up, ferried to the mainland on a barge, and sold to buffalo ranches elsewhere.

The bison, stampeding, were featured in a movie called *The Covered Wagon* that was staged on the island in 1922. Some war scenes, sans bison, were also filmed on the western shore of the lake during World War II for a film called *Wake Island*.

When Antelope Island was visited in 1845 by Captain John C. Frémont (on horseback, as the lake was low), its chief population was a herd of pronghorn antelope. By the 1870s the pronghorns had all disappeared, hunted to extinction or escaping to the main-

Part of the large herd of bison (buffalo) that roam at large on Antelope Island.

land during periods of low water. As funds become available in the future, plans call for reestablishing these fleet-footed animals, along with elk, bighorn sheep, and turkeys. A small deer herd already resides there.

On an earlier expedition in 1843, Frémont, Kit Carson, and three others had paddled a leaky, inflatable "India rubber" boat out to a neighboring island a few miles to the north which Frémont named "Disappointment Island" because of its barrenness. Captain Howard Stansbury, first to circle the entire lake, changed the name to Fremont Island in 1850. Stansbury, of the U.S. Army's Corps of Topographical Engineers, set up a base camp on Antelope Island in 1850 while he conducted his detailed survey of the lake and its islands. Stansbury Island in the southwestern part of the lake bears his name. Like Antelope, it is surmounted by a rocky peak that rises almost 2,500 feet above the lake.

Because of its proximity to Salt Lake City, Antelope Island attracted visitors soon after the first Mormons arrived in the area. Brigham Young and others grazed stock there (it was usually called

Church Island then), and guests were entertained at sometimes lavish weekend parties. Some of the horses eventually grew wild and were occasionally rounded up to be broken for mainland use. Until fairly recent times, both sheep and goats were grazed on the island to the great detriment of its herbage.

The lone grave on the island commemorates a turn-of-the-century tragedy. A herder named George Frary lived there in the 1890s with his wife and six children. When his wife became ill with appendicitis in 1897, Frary sailed to the mainland to seek medical help in the teeth of gale-force winds. Before he could return with a doctor, the appendix ruptured and Mrs. Frary died. Her lonely grave has been maintained ever since by ranchers and more recently by park personnel.

Frary stayed on, raised his family, and devoted years to exploring the lake and taking depth soundings. His figures were used by railroad engineers in laying out the route of the Lucin Cutoff in 1902, and one of his daughters was a passenger on the first train to cross the lake in 1903. It was Frary's cattle boat that was used to haul the original herd of twelve bison, one at a time, to the island.

If one accepts the dictionary definition of an island as "a tract of land smaller than a continent surrounded by water," the Great Salt Lake has nearly a dozen islands at high water. At low water, most of them tend to become peninsulas of sorts, attached to other islands or to the mainland by sandbars, narrow rocky spines, or mud flats. In 1850 Stansbury was able to drive wagons to Antelope Island, and it was possible to ride out to Antelope Island on a horse during the early years of this century, again in the period 1935-40, and in 1964.

Besides Fremont and Stansbury islands, the lake's other major islands are Gunnison, 163 acres, named for Captain Stansbury's chief assistant, Lieutenant John W. Gunnison (*see* Green River State Park), and Carrington, 1,767 acres, named by Captain Stansbury for Albert Carrington, a Mormon church official who assisted in the 1850 survey.

Then there is Bird Island, also known as Hat Island from its shape, inhabited mainly by seagulls. Tiny Egg Island and White Rock, near Antelope Island, also are rookeries for gulls and other migratory birds. Eight miles north of Fremont Island is a muddy twenty-two-acre sandbar called Mud Island, which barely shows above water when the lake is high. The same is true of Badger

Antelope Island's rocky summit shows its volcanic origin.

Island, between Stansbury and Carrington. Strongs Knob adjoins
the railroad causeway and usually is no more than a rocky peninsula. At the far northern end of the lake are two small and barren
islets called Dolphin Island and Cub Island. When the lake is low,
Cub Island is attached to Gunnison Island; Dolphin, to the mainland.

The Great Salt Lake remains one of the most mysterious
regions in the West. So salty at average water levels that a swim-
mer can, as the tourist literature used to say, "float like a cork,"
the lake usually supports only two kinds of life: tiny crustaceans
called brine shrimp that are harvested as feed for tropical fish
aquariums, and a little gnat-like insect called the brine fly, which
clusters in mats along the shores of the lake and swarms in great
numbers during July. Stansbury encountered "cakes" of the
decomposing larvae of the brine fly and found it "nauseous both
to the sight & smell." As water levels increased in recent years,
however, biologists were delighted to discover that a tiny fish called
the rain-water killifish had taken up residence in a part of the lake
where warm-water springs dilute the salinity.

Except for the Great Lakes, the Great Salt Lake is the largest

Domestic cattle at long-abandoned sheds at top of Antelope Island.

natural inland body of water in the United States. It has no outlet,
and its extreme saltiness (two to four times that of the ocean when
the lake is at normal levels) is caused by the evaporation of lake
waters and the concentration of salts over thousands of years.
Only the Dead Sea is saltier. Minerals, including salt, magnesium,
and potash, are extracted from evaporation ponds along the shores
of the lake. Seen from the air, the lake is divided in two by the
Southern Pacific Railroad's Lucin Cutoff, and the color of the
water north and south of the railroad causeway is distinctly different. Along the south shore, additional concentration of the
minerals in the water of the evaporation ponds produces vivid
coloration. Formerly home to thousands of waterfowl until the
rising waters destroyed the complex of dikes and canals that gave
them nesting and feeding grounds, the Great Salt Lake may
decline enough to again offer them refuge. Or, if water levels rise,
and the lake threatens to flood the runways of Salt Lake City
International Airport or send its heavy waves cascading over Interstate 80, Antelope Island will again be isolated, province only of
the bison and the deer.

Bear Lake, a favorite sailing and boating venue.

14

Bear Lake State Park

Bear Lake Marina

Open all year
Camping, 15 units
Picnicing
Group pavilion
Visitor center/museum
Drinking water

Modern restrooms, wheelchair
  accessible
Showers
Sewage disposal
Boating/fishing
Swimming

Freshwater lake, 71,000 surface acres; boating; sailing; swimming; year-round fishing.

Rendezvous Beach

Open May-October
Camping, 138 units
Group camping
Picnicing
Drinking Water
Modern restrooms, wheelchair
  accessible

Showers
Sewage disposal
Utility hookups
Boating/fishing
Swimming
Concessionaire

Wide, sandy beach; picnicing, camping, swimming; small watercraft activity.

East Side — Cisco Beach

Open all year
Primitive camping
Vault toilets
Boating/fishing

Off-highway vehicles allowed
  nearby
Swimming

Ever since it was established in the early 1960s, Bear Lake State Park has been attracting increasing numbers of visitors despite the lovely blue lake's relative isolation in the far northeast corner of Utah on the Idaho border. Occupying only a small fraction of the lake's forty-eight miles of shoreline, the state park lands still are the only public facilities on the Utah part of the lake, and the only places where any accurate estimate of actual visitor totals can be made.

Historically, the lake has been luring visitors for a variety of reasons for more than 165 years. Originally, Bear Lake was probably called Black Bears Lake by one Donald Mackenzie, explorer for the North West Company of Canada who may have discovered it in 1819 while scouting for fur-bearing animals, largely beaver, to satisfy urban demand for hats. The name later became Bear Lake and subsequently came to be applied to the Bear River and its valley. A giant, red-haired Scot who got along well with the local Indians, Mackenzie hunted for beaver all over the Rocky Mountains in the early 1800s.

Utah's state-operated park lands in the Bear Lake area are Bear Lake Marina, Rendezvous Beach, and Cisco Beach.

Bear Lake Marina. Situated on the west side just north of Garden City on U.S. Highway 89, Bear Lake Marina is well equipped for aquatic recreation including boating, fishing, and water-skiing, its principal uses. A park headquarters building overlooking the marina houses the park's administrative offices, a small museum featuring local fish (*see* below on Fishing in Bear Lake), modern restrooms, and an information desk. The fifteen designated camping sites lack shade and lie adjacent to a large parking lot. There is a paved eighty-foot-wide launching ramp as well as dock spaces for over 200 boats.

Rendezvous Beach. At the south end of the lake on State Route 30, Rendezvous Beach has 138 camping spaces in three locations spread along a mile and a half of lakefront. All three camping areas have modern restrooms with showers and one (Big Creek) has utility hookups. A wide, sandy beach provides excellent swimming opportunities during summer months.

The park also is popular for picnics, nature study, photography, and water skiing. At both the marina and at Rendezvous Beach, all campsites are subject to advance reservation and on summer weekends especially are apt to be full.

The beach is named for the famous rendezvous of fur trappers and Indians held there in the summers of 1827 and 1828. The gatherings were attended by a thousand or more Indians and mountain men including Jedediah Smith in 1827, just returned from the perilous first eastward traverse of the Sierras and the Great Basin by white explorers. There were so many campfires at the south end of the lake at these trading sessions that one observer called the area "a lighted city."

Bear Lake—East Side—Cisco Beach. On the undeveloped east shore across the lake from Garden City, Cisco Beach is a day-use facility accessible from the south end of the lake by an unpaved county road. The beach property provides vault toilets and garbage dumpsters, but no other conveniences, on a no-reservation basis.

Cisco Beach is famous for its midwinter fishing with dip nets for the little seven-inch Bonneville Cisco, a member of the white-fish family. For a week or ten days in late January, when the weather is coldest, swarms of the little fish come to the surface to spawn near the shore. They are easily scooped up by hardy fishermen wading waist-deep in the icy water or through holes chopped in the ice if the lake surface is frozen. The fish are considered by some to be good eating, and are also used for bait. Either an Idaho or Utah fishing license is required.

THE GARDEN CITY STORY

Garden City, largest community on the lake, dates from 1864 when a Mormon apostle named Charles C. Rich built some cabins on the lakeshore to house workers for his flour mill, which was followed by a sawmill, a blacksmith shop, and a wood-processing plant. Rich County was named in his honor.

Garden City's small off-season population of a few hundred inhabitants swells to uncounted thousands during the short and busy summer season. The town, as of 1986, had two small motels, a KOA campground, stores, eating establishments, service stations, a library, and government offices. The town is increasingly hemmed in by burgeoning real-estate developments.

All this development carries a potentially disastrous price tag. Irrigation water laden with nutrients from broad, fertilized farmland above the lake and waste water from boats, towns, and summer colonies along the lake shore seriously threaten the lake's water quality. Close watch over the deleterious effects of what is called eutrophication (reduction of water quality, largely through the growth of algae nourished by pollution) is being maintained by the Bear River Regional Commission, funded in part by the federal Environmental Protection Agency, the state of Utah, and the state of Idaho. A positive step is the recent installation of a $4.5 million sewer system to serve part of the west shore in and around

Historical marker at Bear Lake State Park.

Garden City, but much still has to be done to prevent the lake from becoming a victim of its own popularity.

THE BEAR LAKE STORY

Geologists believe that in ancient times the Bear River ran into and out of the north end of what is now Bear Lake through a vast system of swamps of which a remnant is Dingle marsh, next to Mud Lake in the Bear River National Wildlife Refuge. Then about eight or ten thousand years ago, a series of upheavals along the eastern side of the lake created the Bear River Plateau, which diverted the river away from the lake to its present course. The lake became a stable ecological system, its losses from evaporation and percolation balanced by precipitation and inflow from six or eight small local streams. So it remained until modern times host to enormous flocks of migratory waterfowl and myriad other birds and animals. Until state game laws curbed the practice, hunters bragged of taking wagonloads of ducks, geese, sandhill cranes, egrets, herons, and anything else their scatterguns could reach.

Nowadays the lake is again connected to the river, but not naturally. A two-way, man-made canal system brings excess Bear River water into the lake from Mud Lake, which in turn is connected with the river. When the river level goes down during the summer, the flow is reversed, similar to the system employed at Willard Bay (*see* Willard Bay State Park).

Although it meanders some 375 miles through parts of three states, the Bear River ends less than a hundred miles from where it starts, its course a complete horseshoe. Rising high in the Uinta Mountains east of Salt Lake City, the stream wanders northward in and out of western Wyoming, passing east of Bear Lake to enter Idaho. At Soda Springs, between Montpelier and Pocatello, it is turned back southward by a lava barrier, reenters Utah, and finally loses itself in the Bear River Migratory Bird Refuge on the northeastern edge of the Great Salt Lake west of Brigham City.

FISHING IN BEAR LAKE

Bear Lake has long been justly famous for its fishing, particularly for cutthroat and lake trout and whitefish, three of the fifteen species known to exist in the lake and in neighboring Mud Lake. Of the three, only the cutthroat is a true native. In fact, it is Utah's only native trout species. Locally the Bear Lake variety of cutthroat is called Blue Nose because of the color of its head when it is exposed to cold air.

Local fishing boat operators claim that lake trout up to thirty-two pounds, cutthroat up to fifteen pounds, and rainbows up to eight pounds have been caught, but they make no guarantee of such results from a day's charter.

According to a graphic exhibit in the visitor center at Bear Lake Marina, half a million five-inch cutthroat are planted in the lake each season by the Utah Division of Wildlife Resources. Hatched and reared for a year in the state fish hatchery at Mantua, they are released into the lake when they are large enough to survive on their own.

The fish are marked with fluorescent dye that is embedded under the scales. Under ultraviolet light, the dye becomes visible. Biologists can then accumulate data on the age and survival rate of the planted fish.

Lake fishing is permitted all year round with either an Idaho or

Bear Lake yacht harbor, with ranger station and museum in foreground.

a Utah license valid anywhere on the lake. Best results are obtained from using large spoons or Daredevil lures in November and December, bait (cisco or dead sculpin) in April and May, and from deep trolling any time of the year. A deep trough off the east shore provides outstanding fishing for large cutthroat and lake trout, particularly in late spring.

THE LEGENDARY BEAR LAKE MONSTER

As might be expected from a large, remote lake 200 feet deep and not yet entirely spoiled by civilization, Bear Lake has (or had) its resident monster, although there have been no sightings for quite a while. According to the Shoshone Indians of the region, a great beast once lived in the lake, preying on buffalo (bison) that came to drink at the water's edge. But when all the bison perished in a great snowstorm in the 1830s, the monster vanished, or so the story goes.

However, in 1868 a Salt Lake City newspaper reported that "reliable persons" had on several occasions seen a huge creature, measuring perhaps forty feet in length, swimming at great speed, "faster than a horse could run on land." One such report said the monster had a head with "ears or bunches on the side of its head nearly as large as a pint cup" (which doesn't sound very big). The beast, naturally, was accused of carrying off unwary swimmers, young females preferred. Similar creatures were sighted in Utah Lake and the Great Salt Lake in the 1860s and '70s, leaving unanswered the question of whether the monster might be migrating along underground streams.

Not about to pass up such a juicy morsel, the local chamber of commerce now publishes a newsletter adorned with an artist's rendering of the subject, mentioning that it is about 200 feet long, has huge red eyes, and swims at sixty miles an hour. Jet-propelled, no doubt.

Big Sand State Park

Open all year   Vault toilets
Camping (undeveloped)   Boating/fishing
Drinking water   Swimming
Fishing; boating; primitive campground.

In northeastern Utah, within the boundaries of the Uintah and
Ouray Indian Reservation, State Route 87 circles north and east,
from Duchesne on U.S. Highway 40 to between Myton and
Roosevelt. It passes along the way the unpaved entrance road to
Big Sand State Park, which is very easy to miss.

The little park consists of some primitive facilities operated by
a concessionaire beside the dam that forms Big Sand Wash Reservoir. A small impoundment near the hamlet of Upalco, the lake is
used for fishing, boating, and water-skiing in summer, and for
occasional winter ice fishing. There is a paved boat-launching
ramp.

An eighty-four acre tract of land was donated to the state for
recreational purposes in 1964 by the Moon Lake Water Users
Association. An earth-and-rock dam 112-feet high was erected
during the next three years to form a 390-acre lake with a capacity
of 12,000 acre feet of water. The lake is stocked with trout by the
State Division of Wildlife Resources.

The region is high plateau country — just under 6,000 feet
above sea level at the lake — dotted with farms, tiny villages, and
numerous oil and gas wells. A few miles to the north are the
southern access routes to the High Uintas Primitive Area surrounding Utah's highest mountain, 13,528-foot Kings Peak.

Until 1986, the park was part of a checkerboard pattern of
private and government land within the greater boundaries of the
Uintah and Ouray Indian Reservation, domain of the Ute tribe.
All of that changed, however, when the United States Supreme
Court upheld a ruling by a district court in Denver that restored
three million acres of land to the reservation.

Originally, the Utes had been awarded two huge tracts of land,
each about two million acres in size. They were called the Uintah

Reservation, mostly in Duchesne County and set aside in 1861, and the Uncompahgre Reservation, established in 1882 and located mostly in Uintah County. As time passed large portions of this land were withdrawn. One million acres went to the Uinta National Forest, and most of the rest was sold or traded to private individuals, mostly non-Indians. Despite some meager additions, by the twentieth century the reservation had dwindled to about a million acres.

After the Supreme Court decision, tension between Utes and non-Indians increased on the reservation, the second largest in the country. Anglo landowners feared that they would lose their land or be unfairly treated, but gradually the two sides have begun discussions and no major changes in law enforcement, hunting and fishing regulations, water rights, taxation, or land ownership seem imminent. The tribe has proposed, however, severance tax on oil and gas produced on the reservation.

Now fully restored, the old Stagecoach Inn was Fairfield's only respectable hostelry during the town's military regime.

Camp Floyd–Stagecoach Inn State Park

Open March-November   Museum
Day-use only   Drinking water
Picnicing   Modern restrooms, wheelchair
                             accessible

Military cemetery; restored Stagecoach Inn museum; interpretive tours; picnic area.

It may be difficult for the first-time visitor to this unusual little forty-acre state park to accept the fact that for thirty-seven months it was the site of the nation's largest military encampment and Utah's second largest community.

The West is sprinkled with the ghosts of boom-and-bust mining camps that exploded overnight from sagebrush flats into riproaring towns of multiple thousands, then quickly vanished into dust. But Camp Floyd was no mining camp, and although it died as abruptly as it was born, it left no gaunt headframes, no deep holes in the ground, no tailings heaps and slag dumps. In fact, only a fine old hotel, a barn, a military cemetery, and several historical markers remain to tell the camp's remarkable and confusing story.

The state park's headquarters, visitor center, and principal structure is a fully restored, 130-year-old frame-and-adobe hotel called Stagecoach Inn. Across the street, the main thoroughfare in the tiny village of Fairfield, stands a renovated barn that once served as an army commissary, all that remains today of between 300 and 400 military structures. Half a mile to the northwest is a miliary cemetery where rest the bodies of eighty-four officers and men. The cemetery was restored in 1959 by the American Legion and the Utah State Historical Society.

Also known as Carson Inn, Stagecoach Inn was built in 1858 by a Fairfield settler named John Carson as the town's only respectable hostelry. It was also the depot for the Overland Stage Company, which passed through Fairfield from 1858 until the transcontinental railroad was completed through Utah in 1869. It was a Pony express station as well from April 3, 1860, to October 28, 1861, when the telegraph put it out of business.

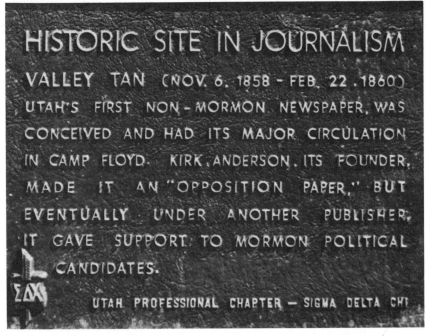

Historic plaque at Camp Floyd State Park.

A devout Mormon, Carson permitted in his establishment none of the bawdy behavior that characterized the rest of the town with its seventeen saloons and numerous houses of ill repute. As one observer put it, Carson maintained "an island of morality in a sea of iniquity." Only square dancing was allowed, and no liquor was served. Nevertheless, many well-known actresses and actors of the time stopped there overnight on their way by Overland Stage to and from San Francisco.

Interpretive tours of the old hotel are conducted during daylight hours from March to November. There are no overnight accommodations in the village. There is a tree-shaded picnic area with restrooms on the spacious lawn behind the hotel.

Along the street in front of the old commissary building stand several monuments with inscriptions relating facts about the place. One bronze plaque commemorates a "historic site in journalism," where Utah's first non-Mormon newspaper, *The Valley Tan*, was printed from November 1858 to February 1860. Catering to the military, the paper at first editorially opposed the Mormon establishment, but later it supported a Mormon candidate for public office. According to Wallace Stegner's *Mormon Country*, "Valley Tan" was a term of derision derived from a name for inferior grades of leather, later a blanket epithet for anything homemade and therefore inferior. In particular, it was applied to a singularly destructive variety of whiskey, also known as "leopard sweat," and to some inferior wine made in southern Utah for sale to gentile (non-Mormon) emigrants and miners.

Another plaque gives some of the history of Fairfield from its origin in 1855 as a walled fort sixty-six-feet square built by Carson and other pioneer settlers. Still another memorializes Colonel Philip St. George Cooke, whom it refers to as "an impartial friend, humanitarian, [and] soldier dedicated to the West." As the last commanding officer at Camp Floyd, Cooke changed the name to Fort Crittenden on February 6, 1861, apparently after General Thomas Crittenden of the Union Army's 32nd Infantry. Secretary of War John B. Floyd, for whom the camp originally had been named, had defected to the Confederacy. This command was not Colonel Cooke's first experience with Mormons. In 1846, a year before the founding of Salt Lake City, Cooke was assigned to lead a detachment of 500 Mormon volunteers assigned to fight in the Mexican War. They enlisted with the proviso that they be allowed to settle somewhere in the West after the war, a scheme ascribed to Brigham Young. Although they made a dramatic march overland from Iowa to Santa Fe (where Cooke took command) and thence to San Diego, the only action they saw was against a herd of wild bulls on the San Pedro River in Arizona. A dozen men were injured before the bulls were shot or driven off. Cooke's "Mormon Battalion" did map out a feasible wagon route along the southern border that was followed by some of the Forty-niners during the California gold rush.

Why the army left Fairfield in a hurry is clear enough—it was called back to active duty when the Civil War broke out. Why it came there is the first place is not as clear. In fact, there is a library shelf full of books on the subject, and they do not all agree. (One interesting account of traveling with the army is *To Utah with the Dragoons, and Glimpses of Life in Arizona and California, 1858-59*). It may be sufficient to state that President Buchanan was led to believe, in 1857, that the Mormons of Utah were on the verge of armed rebellion against the United States government. The president accordingly ordered an army detachment from Fort Leavenworth, Kansas, to march to Utah and suppress the alleged revolt.

A formidable force headed west with 3,500 men, 586 horses, 500 wagons, and 3,000 mules — infantry, cavalry, artillery, engineers, ambulances, supply trains, and several brass bands. However, before the army reached Utah, orders arrived from Washington that the Mormons were not to be molested in any way whatever, unless they showed outright armed resistance.

Cooler heads had prevailed. The president was told that Brigham Young, despite some warlike proclamations, would not actually oppose the invasion force if it turned out to be entirely peaceful and *if* it did not tarry in or near Salt Lake City.

After wintering at Fort Bridger, Wyoming, the detachment under Brevet Brigadier General Albert Sidney Johnston emerged from the Wasatch Mountains through Emigration Canyon on June 25, 1858, and then marched right though Salt Lake City without incident. There was almost nobody there. Not trusting the invading gentiles, Brigham Young had ordered the city abandoned, leaving only a few men with torches ready to set fire to the capital if there should be any sign of hostility from the troops. Even the foundations of the Mormon Temple, then in the early stages of construction, were buried to resemble a plowed field.

But nothing untoward happened, and the army arrived at Fairfield on July 8. The place would never again be the same. The sheer logistics of the military encampment are staggering in retrospect. Once in camp, Johnston's army could not live off the land and had to rely for food and supplies on a continuous caravan from Fort Leavenworth more than 1,100 miles away, with much of the route controlled by hostile Indians. A civilian contractor, the firm of Russell, Majors & Waddell, was hired to haul some 10 million pounds of freight to the new encampment. Alexander Majors later recalled in *Seventy Years on the Frontier* that for the year 1858 Russell, Majors & Waddell used 3,500 wagons, 40,000 oxen, and employed 4,000 men — and much of this was used to supply the soldiers.

Hard on the heels of the army, of course, came the usual horde of artisans, mechanics, and tradespeople, and just as inevitably saloonkeepers, gamblers, con artists, robbers, thieves, and prostitutes. Camp Floyd was populated by several thousand men a long way from home, and it also had the only hard currency in the

Rocky Mountain West. Here was gold that did not have to be dug out of the ground the hard way.

But then the Civil War began and the army was needed elsewhere. All the camp buildings — warehouses, barracks, mess halls, shops, and stables — were either dismantled and hauled away by the eager civilians or burned along with a huge pile of munitions and weaponry. The latter, accumulated over a three-year period, was too bulky and too dangerous to be hauled back in a hurry and could not be allowed to fall into Confederate hands. Surplus military stores valued at $4,000,000 were sold at auction for a few cents on the dollar, and the foundations for the fortunes of some merchants were laid with this sale.

The grand explosion that destroyed most of the remaining ammunition and guns celebrated the end of Camp Floyd and of Fairfield as a boom town. By September 2, 1862, the village had shrunk to just eighteen families, not counting the eighty-four officers and enlisted men sleeping in the military cemetery.

Coral Pink Sand Dunes. Photograph courtesy of Utah Travel Council.

Coral Pink Sand Dunes State Park

Open April-November
Camping, 22 units
Group pavilion
Drinking water
Modern restrooms, wheelchair accessible
Vault toilets
Showers
Sewage disposal
Off-highway vehicles permitted

Pink sand dunes; camping; off-highway vehicle riding; exploring; photography.

Although it is somewhat off the beaten track, the natural attractions and easy access of this park near Kanab in southwestern Utah lure upwards of 80,000 visitors a year, mostly in summer.

Parts of the 3,730-acre park are designated for off-road vehicles, to be found there almost any weekend or holiday, weather permitting. A dune-buggy rally each Fourth of July draws enthusiasts from all over the West to race hell-for-leather over the rolling dunes. The rest of the dunes are the haunt of hikers, nature lovers, painters, and photographers. At dawn and at sunset the dunes take on rich copper hues deepening to magenta, and fantastic shadow patterns accent the scene. The dunes occupy about 2,000 acres of the park at an elevation of 6,000 feet above sea level; the rest of the park is typical foothill juniper and piñon country with some steep cliffs and rocky outcroppings. The tract was acquired from the federal Bureau of Land Management in 1963 for $9,325.

A modern campground adjoining the dunes has twenty-two campsites in a dense grove of trees. Each site has a cooking grill, firepit, picnic tables, concrete slab, and garbage can. There are flush toilets and hot showers in a central restroom facility. There are no hookups, but fresh-water taps are scattered through the campground. From late October until Easter, the water is turned off and the restrooms closed, but two pit toilets are maintained nearby. In season, firewood and ice are for sale in the park.

Rail fence made of aspen casts strong shadow in early morning light at Coral Pink Sand Dunes State Park.

Sand—Much Ado About Practically Nothing*

Long ago I fell in love with sand dunes, not to race over in a dune buggy, but to wander through, sit upon, or meditate about. Have you ever really stopped to think about sand, in or out of a dune, except on a picnic when it seasoned your sandwich or filled your shoes or bogged your vehicle down to its axles?

If and when you do ponder on it, you will find that sand is a curiously contradictory substance; formless but unyielding, ephemeral but enduring. Worthless as a commodity *in situ*, it is outrageously expensive to move in any quantity to where you want it.

Sand is primeval, having been around since the planet was young, yet it has become as essential to present-day living as soap, the integrated circuit, and TV serials. Sand is an irreplaceable ingredient in every concrete structure, in glass, and in pottery. With sand you tell time, make mortar, form castings, etch metal, dam up a river, divert a flood, decorate your patio, build a castle on a beach, smooth a rough surface or roughen a smooth one.

Sand is terrible in your hair, your teeth, your contact lenses, your camera shutter, or your bed, but it is wonderful under your bare feet when it is damp and cool. By the handful sand is nothing, mere grist from the interminable churning of the elements. By the dune-full, sand can be incredibly, mysteriously beautiful, home to a whole universe of tiny living creatures but by and large as aloof as the sea to man's intruding.

Sand Dunes: Windblown Wonderlands

Noteworthy sand dunes are found in almost every state and along every seashore, but except for those piled up by ocean waves, they are all creatures of the wind. Some such heaps, like those at Sand Mountain in central Nevada, attain a height of a thousand feet or more. The massive dunes at Great Sand Dunes National Monument in Colorado are supplied constantly from the

---

*Portions of this essay appeared in *Westways* in January 1967.

wide, dry shores of the Rio Grande River in the San Luis Valley, twenty-odd miles to the southwest.

Similarly, Utah's Coral Pink Sand Dunes are built of sand carried by the prevailing wind from the Virgin River bottoms to Cane Beds, just over the state line in Arizona. Their brilliant reddish hue, incidentally, is from iron oxide.

The ability that sand has to pile up in such large heaps, and the peculiar geometric shapes of the dune crests and slopes, seem to be functions of the shape and size of the sand particles or grains in a particular dune. The sand in Death Valley dunes in California is so fine it runs through your fingers like water. The same characteristics no doubt account for the varied and wonderful sounds emitted by some dunes under pressure of the wind or the human foot or for no apparent reason at all. The rubbing of grain against grain, magnified some astronomical number of times, is the simplest explanation for the moans and groans, the whispers and sighs, and the bumping noises heard at some dunes.

The dunes at Nevada's Sand Mountain clearly sing sometimes, accounting for their earlier name, "The Singing Sands." The Barking Sands of Kauai, Rumbling Mountain in Chile, and the Hill of the Bells on the Sinai Peninsula doubtless owe their acoustical properties to the same phenomenon.

But I prefer the explanation offered by some primitive peoples. Closer to nature than we, they believe that the dunes hold imprisoned the spirits of the departed who are crying out for rescue. If such is the case, the spirits must be buried pretty deep or they could easily get out through the holes made by the living dwellers of the dunes, whose numbers are legion.

It has been said that sand has a memory like that of a simple computer — a brief memory for transient events, a longer memory for deeper impressions. Indeed, the smooth surface of a dune can provide each calm morning a record of the events of the night before. Radiating from bushes and shrubs and the roots of junipers, from burrows and crevices and cracks in the rocks, multitudes of tiny tracks may be discerned. The number and variety of tracks will astonish the uninitiated, crisscrossing and overlapping, some ending abruptly in flurried signs of tragedy. But let a breeze come and the tracks will vanish, all save the ones deeply scoured by jeeps, dune bikes, or other mechanical intruders. Given time, even those wounds will heal themselves.

Dunes are the home of moles, voles, shrews, and mice, of plume-tailed kangaroo rats, of rabbits and ground squirrels and skunks and wildcats and coyotes, of lizards and snakes and fleas and flies and scorpions and centipedes and many kinds of worms, or hawks and crows and ravens and sparrows. Most of them show a remarkable adaptation to their sandy living conditions. The resident mice of White Sands National Monument in New Mexico, for example, are white, while their neighbors of the same species in the lava beds to the north are black or brown.

Odd though it may seem, seeds are the basic food of most of the smaller creatures dwelling in the dunes. Many of them never drink water, extracting what moisture they need from their food. And these animals in turn provide food for the rest of the crowd right on up to the largest of the predators. Where do all these seeds come from? From flowers, of all things. Once in every several years, or decades, when the right amount of rain falls in the right place at the right time — in the spring before the early summer heat begins — seeds that have survived deep in the sand burst forth in ephemeral bloom, covering the sand with solid masses of flaming color right up to the slopes of the shifting dunes.

Some of the flowers that bloom among the dunes are so tiny they can be examined only by lying on one's stomach (which is why they are called "belly flowers"). There is even a Belly Flower Club in Southern California devoted to the scrutiny and photography of such Lilliputian blossoms. On the other hand, some flowers like the lupine attain the size of bushes.

But after their brief and brave show, a matter of hours or days or perhaps a few weeks at best, they fade, wither, and die and soon disappear entirely — but not before they have produced a crop of seeds to feed the denizens of the dunes. This work was done with man's assistance in San Francisco's coastal dune area, where Golden Gate Park now lies. There ryegrass, then lupine, and finally trees and shrubs were planted in succession over a period of decades on land that had been considered by developers to be worthless.

Even without trees or shrubs or flowers, dunes come in many colors, like the soft pastels in and around Coral Pink Sand Dunes, the lovely orange-hued sand of Canyon de Chelly National Monument in Arizona, or the shining silver of Nevada's Sand Mountain.

Hiker following crest of dune in Coral Pink Sand Dunes State Park.

Colored sands have been used for generations by the Navajo for the famous sand paintings used in religious ceremonies. The jade-green and coal-black sand of the Big Island of Hawaii are tourist attractions. And even the drabbest, most ordinary dune can be transformed by late afternoon or early morning light into a marvel of magenta and copper and bronze.

Epilogue

Even if you are not a naturalist, a geologist, an artist, or a photographer, an hour spent wandering among or sitting upon sand dunes can be richly rewarding almost any time of day, but especially at dawn. You may fix your eyes on the ground to learn the tidings of the hidden inhabitants, rest your gaze on the marvelously clean lines of the dune crests against the sky, or listen to the mysterious music from all around you.

In the dunes, if you will calm your mind and compose your spirit, you may hear the musical breath of nature in the susurrus of wind over sand. You may, if you have patience, witness the infinitely painstaking process by which the dunes move inexorably, grain by grain, through the intricate figure of their cosmic dance.

For it is the destiny of the dunes never to be the same from one hour to the next, nor from one day to another, yet never to have changed at all in a thousand years. This, perhaps, is the essence of their magic: that pervasive sense of timelessness that nothing can dispel.

Always in the dunes, in the words of desert writer Mary Austin, there is room enough and time enough.

View of serpentine Colorado River from Dead Horse Point State Park overlook.

38

Dead Horse Point State Park

Open all year
Camping, 21 units
Group camping
Picnicing
Visitor center
Drinking water

Modern restrooms, wheelchair
  accessible
Sewage disposal
Utility hookups, electricity only
Off-highway vehicles

2,000 feet above the Colorado River; photography; panoramic view of the Colorado River

Hang gliding and mustang roping would not seem to have much in common, give or take a century, but the high, narrow mesa now occupied by Dead Horse Point State Park in southeastern Utah happens to be singularly well suited for both activities.

The wild horse roundups responsible for the name of the point and the park stopped a long time ago, and hang gliding is in its comparative infancy there. But the extraordinary scenery that is the park's number one attraction has been there for millions of years, and the canyon-carving process that created the scene continues as if men had never found the place.

Meanwhile the visitors come, 100,000 a year at last count, nearly all of them drawn by the view. Those who take the time to read the park's brochure, or to stroll the paths and read the signs, discover for themselves why such a fascinating place is burdened with such a lugubrious title.

Perhaps in its details the story might suffer from close inspection, or perhaps the truth is worse than the accepted version, but it is worth reporting even if only a legend. As the story goes, cowboys before the turn of the century (and before the A.S.P.C.A.) used the long, narrow point where the park is now situated as a holding ground for wild horses. Since the sheer-sided mesa has a narrow neck only thirty yards wide, it was easily fenced after the mustangs, rounded up on their nearby feeding grounds, had been herded out onto the point.

There the best of the lot were roped, branded, and broken, and the rest left to their own devices. Accounts differ as to just what happened next. Some say the remaining mustangs were simply abandoned by the cowboys, who may or may not have assumed the nags would soon find their way back to the rest of the wild herd.

Others assert that the cowboys deliberately left the fence in place to keep the animals from rejoining the herd, regarding the broomtails as "vermin not worth shooting." The mustangers, as they were called, were not known for being humane.

In either case, the result was the same. The frantic horses left on the point, unable or unwilling to try to find their way out, soon died of thirst and exhaustion. There was no water on their rocky prison, and there still is none except for what is hauled in from thirty-two miles away by the park's tank trucks. Rainfall averages only about eight inches a year, and it quickly runs off or evaporates.

Oh, there is water aplenty in plain sight, 2,000 feet or more down below in the muddy brown Colorado River, but only a bird or one of those hang-glider pilots can reach it directly, for most of the short way is vertical. No doubt some of the wild horses died attempting to reach the river.

Nowadays the scene that spelled death to the mustangs is one of the park's major attractions. The view from the point, where the hang gliders take off, is simply stupendous. The La Sal Mountains provide a backdrop for a fantastic tangle of buttes and pinnacles and mesas in contrasting shades of yellow and red and purple sandstone, through which the serpentine Colorado River threads its meandering way. Jeep trails zigzag down into the rockbound maze of Canyonlands National Park to the south and west, where the Green River joins the Colorado at the head of Cataract Canyon.

Dead Horse Point has been a state park since 1959, acquired a parcel at a time, first by donation from San Juan County, and later by trade or purchase from the Utah State Land Board and the federal Bureau of Land Management. In land area the park now totals 5,082 acres, most of it about 6,000 feet above sea level.

Particularly in May, June and September, the main campground's twenty-one fully developed units—subject to advance reservation—are apt to be full by late afternoon. Each drive-in unit has a shelter with electrical hookup, grill, table and benches, and a tent pad. The park has a modern central restroom but no showers. Piped water is available at several places, and there is an RV dump station.

Nearby is an overflow campground, also available for groups by reservation, which has pit toilets, grills, and tables, but not water. There is also a day-use picnic area with twelve sites. Gathering firewood is prohibited, but bundled firewood is for sale at the visitor center. Winter camping is allowed at the park's picnic area. The restroom is kept open all winter unless the water line supplying it freezes.

Year round, park records show that only about 11 percent of the visitors are overnight campers. The rest come to picnic, walk the trails, observe the wildlife and wildflowers in season, or to watch the hang gliders on the relatively rare occasions when they are aloft. Special use permits may be obtained for such activities as weddings, dances, art exhibits, movie making, and rock climbing.

A paved walking trail one and one-half miles long starts at the visitor center and runs out along the point, which also is accessible by paved road. Seven miles of hiking trails beckon more ambitious hikers, who are warned to carry water. Also at the large and attractive visitor center near the entrance are restrooms, an amphitheater for evening programs during the busy season, interpretive exhibits, an information desk where literature may be obtained, the park's administrative offices, and a first-aid room.

Meanwhile, down in the canyon, the mills of the gods grind on ever so slowly but as inexorably as they have for eons. As the park brochure states succinctly, "From the overlook, canyon erosion may be viewed on a grand scale. This erosion process has taken approximately 150 million years. Much of it is caused by the river slicing down into the earth's crust as land is forced upward. These powerful forces are still sculpturing the fantastic shapes of these precipitous cliffs and towering spires."

Quiet cove attracts boaters at Deer Creek State Park.

Deer Creek State Park

Open April-November   Showers
Camping, 23 units   Sewage disposal
Group camping   Boating/fishing
Picnicking   Swimming
Drinking water   Concessionaire
Modern restrooms, wheelchair accessible
Sailing; sailboarding; scenic mountain views; year-round fishing

Seven miles long and half a mile wide, more or less, Deer Creek
Reservoir on the Provo River eight miles southwest of Heber City
has long been one of Utah's most popular lakes for year-round
recreation, largely because of its proximity to the Wasatch Front.
Long a popular spot for fishing, boating, water-skiing, and ice
fishing, in recent years the lake has become Utah's wind-surfing
capital because of its reliable up-canyon afternoon winds.

Established in 1971, the 3,260-acre state park includes all of
the lake's surface and a narrow strip of leased land along its eastern shore. Park facilities include a fully-equipped campground.
There are also several smaller state park camping and fishing
access sites, and one large privately owned camping facility with
RV hookups. Also, the park has a concrete launching ramp,
docks, and a boat storage yard.

Constructed between 1938 and 1940 as a federal works project,
Deer Creek Dam is an earth-fill structure 235 feet high and 1,304
feet long at the top. The dam also serves as the crossing for highway U.S. 189 between Heber City and Provo. The reservoir has a
storage capacity of 15,000 acre-feet of water. Along its northwest-
ern shore run the tracks of the steam-powered excursion railroad
called the Heber Creeper, which makes several round trips a day in
season from Heber City to Vivian Park below the reservoir (*see*
Wasatch Mountain State Park).

In addition to its many recreational uses, the reservoir supplies
irrigation, industrial, and culinary water for the valleys below, as
well as for several hydroelectric power plants on the river below the
dam. One of these, known as Olmstead, was built in 1903-4 to

43

Mountains, water, and sun draw summer crowds to Deer Creek State Park.

furnish electric power to the mining camp of Mercur, thirty-five miles away, over one of the nation's first alternating current transmission lines.

Deer Creek Reservoir takes its name from a principal tributary of the Provo River that enters the lake just below the dam. Geographically speaking, the lake might be more accurately named Provo Reservoir, for it is actually just a wide place on the river. Originating in the Wasatch National Forest high country at Trial Lake, the Provo River has its source near the headwaters of three other major river drainages: the Weber, the Bear, and the Duchesne.

From there the Provo flows generally westward through some of Utah's most spectacular mountain scenery and alpine playgrounds, followed much of the way by paved State Route 150. Then at Jordanelle, due north of Heber City, the river makes an abrupt left turn to follow an ancient fault line southward between Heber City and Midway to enter Deer Creek Reservoir near Charleston. In the Heber Valley it serves a vast network of irrigation ditches and canals and is augmented by numerous tributaries. Above and especially below the reservoir, the river remains one of

Utah's finest trout streams, despite continued bickering between fishermen and water and power users over water allocations.

Well before it reaches the Heber Valley, the Provo's flow is increased by a canal from the Weber River, and still higher up in the Wasatch Range by a long tunnel diverting part of the Duchesne River above Cataract Gorge into the Provo. The Weber River canal was built in 1929-30 and was enlarged between 1941 and 1947. The diversion tunnel was completed in 1942, a major engineering project.

In 1987, construction began at Jordanelle on a new dam that will flood about five miles each of the scenic Upper Provo and Ross Creek drainages. Diversion tunnels now connect a number of rivers to the east with the Provo River. All of this activity is part of the Central Utah Project, a forty-year, $2-billion scheme of reservoirs, tunnels, canals, and pumping plants that will shift water from the Green River drainage in eastern Utah to cities, industry, and farms along the Wasatch Front. During the 1980s, the Central Utah Project was bitterly contested, with environmentalists and outdoorsmen labeling it a boondoggle.

Like the city of Provo, the river takes its name not from the usual Indian or Mormon sources but from an early-day French-Canadian fur trapper, Etienne Provost. Based in Taos, New Mexico, Provost first entered the region in 1824. He may have been the first European to sight the Great Salt Lake. Provost returned the following year with a larger party and trapped beaver throughout the area, attending the first of the famous rendezvous of trappers, Indians, and fur traders that summer on the Henry's Fork of the Green River in what is now southern Wyoming.

Looking down East Canyon Lake toward the dam.

46

East Canyon State Park

Open all year
Camping, 31 units
Group camping
Picnicing
Drinking water
Modern restrooms, wheelchair accessible

Showers
Sewage disposal
Boating/fishing
Swimming
Concessionaire

High mountain lake; camping; boating; year-round fishing; close to Salt Lake City

It used to be said of East Canyon Reservoir, twenty-eight miles northeast of Salt Lake City, that on the opening day of the fishing season so many lines and lures were thrown in the lake that its level rose four feet. Now that year-round fishing is permitted, there is no opening day as such, but the weekend crowds can still get pretty thick whenever the weather is favorable.

In fact, upwards of 300,000 visitors a year take advantage of the lake's easy accessibility by State Routes 65 and 66 from Interstates 84 and 80. It was not always thus. The narrow canyon now occupied by a 680-acre reservoir once posed a major obstacle to westward-bound pioneers traveling through the region. The first wagon train to pass through the canyon in 1846 (before the California Gold Rush) needed to hack a rough road through the head-high brush. The delays the party suffered in the canyon later proved tragic and helped to write one of the West's most somber historic tales (*see* The Donner-Reed Story at the end of this chapter).

Established in 1967, East Canyon State Park now occupies 267 acres along the shores of the lake at an elevation of about 5,700 feet above sea level. Its major activities include camping, picnicing, fishing, boating, water-skiing, and swimming, and in winter snowmobiling, ice fishing, and cross-country skiing. In winter, State Route 65 from the south is closed, but routes 65 and 66 from Interstate 84 to the north are kept open. A concession-operated snack bar and boat rental facility offer camping and fishing supplies during the summer season.

There are thirty-one developed campsites at the north end of the lake that have modern restrooms, picnic tables, grills, and piped drinking water, but no showers or trailer hookups. There is a sewage disposal station. A wide, concrete boat-launching ramp adjoins a paved parking area. Two group sites, available by advance reservation, have barbecue pits and shaded pavilions, one with five picnic tables, the other with eleven. In addition, there are 300 overflow campsites along the lake with pit toilets and garbage cans, but no tables, grills, or drinking water.

Originally developed as a local irrigation project in the 1920s, the reservoir has been enlarged three times as part of the Weber Basin Reclamation Project. East Canyon Creek, the lake's principal source, originates near Park City twenty miles to the south and flows northward, eventually joining the Weber River at Morgan.

After the Donner-Reed Party broke trail through the canyon in 1846, the advance guard of the great Mormon emigration passed through in 1847 (*see* Pioneer Trail State Park), followed by most travelers to and through Salt Lake City for the next two decades. Johnston's Army (*see* Camp Floyd-Stagecoach Inn State Park) came that way in 1858, as did the Overland Stage and the Pony Express.

Seldom traversed after 1851, when the Parley's Canyon route now followed by Interstate 80 came into general use, the old wagon trail was followed in places by the first automobiles to venture into the canyon. The abandoned right-of-way of an early logging railroad (1907-17) also was used as a road until the completion of State Route 65 in 1947. Still narrow and winding, the route offers magnificent views of the peaks and canyons of the Wasatch Mountains.

One point in particular, marked by a historical monument, is at 7,420-foot-high Big Mountain Summit. It is one of several such monuments marking the route of the Mormon migration (the so-called "Donner-Mormon Trail") from Fort Bridger, Wyoming, to the site of Pioneer Trail State Park on the eastern border of Salt Lake Valley. It reads:

> On 19 July 1847, scouts Orson Pratt and John Brown climbed the mountain and became the first Latter-day Saints to see the Salt Lake Valley. Due to illness, the pioneer camp had divided into three small companies. On 23 July, the last party, led by Brigham Young,

reached the Big Mountain. By that time most of the first companies were already in the valley and planting crops.

THE DONNER-REED STORY

Roadside markers and monuments all the way from Henefer to the hamlet of Grantsville south of the Great Salt Lake summarize the fate of the Donner-Reed Party. It is a tale that to this day provokes strong argument about just what happened to these California-bound pioneers, and how and why, and who was to blame.

The following account is a condensed version of the story, extracted from various published sources without entering into the controversy any more than necessary. Of Iowa and Illinois stock, the emigrants were farmers lured westward by tales of a land of milk and honey with vast tracts of fertile land free for the taking. Nobody in the party was looking for gold—its discovery in California was still in the future—nor was anyone seemingly concerned (if they knew anything at all about it) that their hopes for the future lay in Mexican territory, whose authorities might not welcome them.

The group became known as the Donner-Reed Party from its principal members, two Donner families and one Reed family, who started out together. Others joined the party along the way knowing there was safety in numbers against hostile Indians. However, the Donners and the Reeds do not appear to have been in charge; perhaps nobody was.

Acting on advice based on claims of an adventurer named Lansford W. Hastings, who had made the journey only once (on horseback and in good weather), eighty-seven men, women, and children in ponderous wagons drawn by oxen left the well-traveled Oregon Trail at Fort Bridger in southwestern Wyoming on July 31, 1846. It was very late in the season for such a venture—as it turned out, fatally late. Seeking to save time on a shorter route, the party headed southwest following the tracks of earlier parties. At the site of present-day Henefer, the emigrants turned southward through the canyon now occupied by East Canyon Reservoir, where they met their first major obstacle in the form of the narrow canyon's rocky defile and its thickets of brush as high as a man's head. The emigrants had to chop their way along a foot at a time, losing skin and clothing and much precious time in the process. The passage took nineteen days, twelve more than were required by the better-organized vanguard of Mormon settlers the following year who were able to use much of the road cut by the Donner-Reed Party.

Finally emerging from Emigration Canyon on the east side of the future site of Salt Lake City, the emigrants continued across the salty desert south of the Great Salt Lake only to discover another exhausting and time-consuming barrier. Where earlier explorers on horseback had found the eighty miles of waterless desert passable, the Donner-Reed Party's heavy wagons and ox teams broke through the crust into deep sand and mud. The three-day crossing killed many of their oxen and so weakened the remainder that they needed nearly a week of precious time to recover.

When they arrived on the banks of the Truckee River at what is now Reno, Nevada, the emigrants might still have avoided disaster had they chosen to pass the winter there. But instead, hoping to make California, they pressed on only to encounter unseasonably early snows in the Sierra Nevada range in the vicinity of the lake now called Tahoe. Sierra Nevada is Spanish for "snowy range," an ominously appropriate term. The party had no way of knowing that they were trying to traverse a region that records some of the world's heaviest snowfalls, measured not in inches but in yards.

They paused at the foot of a high pass, at a place ever since called Donner Lake, while some of the men scouted ahead. More snow caught the main party in camp, buried all traces of the trail, and spelled the doom of nearly half of them. By the time relief arrived, summoned by the five men who had struggled through to the far side of the mountains, the surviving emigrants were in the last stages of starvation. In a final act of desperation, some had resorted to cannibalism. Of the eighty-seven emigrants who had started west, only forty-seven made it all the way, about half of them children—a miracle in itself.

Even the well-equipped relief parties had great difficulty in reaching the scene; it took four different expeditions to rescue all the survivors, including some of the members of the first rescue teams. It was April 1847, a full year from the start of the overland trek, before the last of them reached safety in sunny California.

By that time the United States was at war with Mexico and the discovery of gold at Sutter's Fort was less than a year ahead—a discovery that precipitated the greatest mass movement of people since the Crusades. It may be said that the Donner-Reed Party led the way to California, but at a terrible price.

Edge of the Cedars State Park

Day-use only
Picnicing
Visitor center/museum

Drinking water
Modern restrooms, wheelchair
    accessible

Indian village; museum; excavated dwellings, ceremonial chambers

The rather odd name of this small park in the town of Blanding is derived from the mistaken notion of the Mormon pioneers who settled there in 1905 that the abundant, shrubby trees of the region were cedars. Actually the trees were Utah junipers (*Juniperus utahensis*). The error is still common throughout the West, for although there are no true native cedars in the western hemisphere, many varieties of juniper, cypress, arborvitae, and other species are popularly called cedars and their wood used for chests, shingles, and fence posts.

It was not for the trees themselves but because of their location on a well-watered plateau that the site of Blanding was chosen. Migrating northward from their earlier settlements along the San Juan River, where they were victimized by a series of floods, the pioneer farmers settled on fertile White Mesa overlooking a stream they called Westwater Creek. There they raised hay and grain, cattle and horses, and pinto beans.

They made use of building materials from the prehistoric Indian ruins in the vicinity for their homes, outbuildings, and enclosures, but evidently did little or no excavation of the principal cluster of ruins on the nearby rim of Westwater Canyon.

Julian Steward apparently investigated the site in the late 1920s, but formal excavation of the ruins did not start until late in the 1960s, when an archaeological team from Weber State College at Ogden undertook the task. The work has continued off and on since that time. Portions of the excavated ruins have now been stabilized and are open to visitors on marked trails.

The complex consists of six residential and ceremonial clusters of stone and adobe structures along a ridge directly behind the museum on the east rim of the canyon. The buildings are believed to have been constructed and occupied between about A.D. 700

and 1220. The reason for their abandonment is not known, but may have been due to drought, raids by marauding tribes, or simply population pressures.

An unusual feature of the ruins is the large number of kivas, underground chambers used for various religious and social purposes. There are ten kivas in all, the largest a so-called "Great Kiva," the northernmost one yet discovered.

The ruins were listed on the National Register of Historic Places in 1971, and the 6.65-acre site was donated to the Division of Parks and Recreation in 1975. The imposing two-story stone headquarters and museum building was erected in 1978 to preserve and interpret the 2,000-year history of the region, including that of the ancient Anasazi, the later Ute and Navajo Indians, and the early white settlers.

STORIES OF BLANDING

Blanding was originally called Grayson, after a pioneer settler, but changed its name after an Easterner named Thomas D. Bicknell offered to build a library for any town that would adopt his name. Two Utah towns accepted: Grayson and the tiny village of Thurber in Wayne County. To settle the matter, the library fund was divided, with half going to Thurber, which adopted the name Bicknell. The other half went to Grayson, which then became Blanding, Mrs. Bicknell's maiden name.

The town of Blanding was front-page news briefly in 1923 as the site of what has been called the "last Indian war" in the United States. After years of resentment and minor conflicts between local Paiutes and Utes and the Mormon settlers, two young Indians were arrested for robbing a sheep camp, killing a calf, and burning a bridge. Found guilty, they were awaiting sentencing when one escaped on horseback; the other went with Posey, a tribal leader who had been outspoken about Indian rights. Posey led a group of Indians westward while the remainder of the tribe was locked up in the Blanding schoolhouse. A pursuing posse engaged in a shootout with the fleeing Indians, who escaped after killing a horse and firing a bullet through a Model T that was part of the posse.

Three days later, most of the Indians surrendered and were placed in a makeshift stockade in the center of town. Posey had never been found. Journalists and law-enforcement officials made

Self-guided nature trails lead to prehistoric Indian ruins at Edge of the Cedars State Park.

sensational statements about the "war," but as time dragged on, emotions calmed. Finally Indians in the stockade revealed the whereabouts of Posey, who had probably died from blood poisoning after being wounded in the gunfight. One other Indian had been killed as well.

"Posey's War" eventually resulted in setting aside land for the Indians at White Mesa, south of Blanding, and put an end to the raids on livestock. Indian children were sent away to boarding schools, and one of the last bands of Indians who were free to roam the countryside was confined.

Within a hundred miles of Blanding are uncountable numbers of prehistoric archaeological sites, ranging from tiny granaries beneath inaccessible cliffs to the famous ruins and foundations of structures at Mesa Verde in Colorado, Chaco Canyon in New Mexico, Canyon de Chelly in Arizona, and Hovenweep in Utah. The Four Corners region—so-called because these four states come together at a common point southeast of Blanding—is one of the richest areas in the world for investigating the remnants of prehistoric civilizations. But for generations, the non-Indian residents of the area have been exploring, digging, and recovering artifacts from sites on both private and federally owned land. Some of the baskets, pots, and other remnants uncovered in these ruins have been kept in the families of the finders and passed down from generation to generation. Others, however, have been sold to collectors and museums throughout the world.

With some exceptional pieces of pottery fetching prices of five figures, it is not surprising that this looting of ancient sites has increased dramatically in recent years. While some of these amateur archaeologists are responsible and well meaning (even calling in professionals when noteworthy finds are uncovered), others are in it only for the money. In the worst cases, looters have brought in backhoes and other power equipment and methodically destroyed huge areas in their quest for valuable artifacts. Such activity on federal land is strictly illegal, and in the mid-1980s federal agents conducted a series of well-publicized raids on private homes in the Blanding area, confiscating relics and arresting one person, who was eventually acquitted. Other cases are still pending.

Local residents defend their digging in the ruins as a hobby traditional to the area. Native Americans see the digging as desecrating the graves of their ancestors and robbing them of their rightful heritage. Archaeologists are disturbed by the amateurs' bungling and haste and their disregard for the historic context in which artifacts occur. The Bureau of Land Management and other federal agencies have such limited funds that they have so far been unable to interdict the flow of artifacts out of the area, with valuable sites left looking like a war zone, pocked with craters, littered with rubble, and lost to history forever. Hikers and explorers, needless to say, should look and photograph to their hearts' content, but leave even the smallest shards of pottery untouched, in the same place they've been for hundreds of years.

Dead juniper limb contrasts with sections of petrified log at Escalante State Park.

Escalante State Park

Open all year

Showers

Camping, 21 units

Sewage disposal

Group camping

Boating/fishing

Picnicing

Off-highway vehicles

Drinking water

Swimming

Modern restrooms, wheelchair accessible

Petrified wood; mineralized dinosaur bones; camping; water-oriented activities; hiking.

The ancient Anasazi and later the Paiute Indians who camped and hunted in the area now called Escalante State Park doubtless had their own mystical explanation for the origin of all those rainbow-hued logs and dinosaur bones cast in hard rock. Unfortunately, their explanations were never recorded. Today's scientific theories about these widespread deposits of mineralized wood and bone are less mystical but perhaps no less difficult for the casual visitor to accept.

Until 1986, the place was called the Escalante Petrified Forest, a name which at least said something about the park's main reason for being. Originally established in 1963, the 1,784-acre park lies just outside the ranching and tourist town of Escalante on State Route 54 about forty miles east of Bryce Canyon National Park. A paved route northward through the village of Boulder connects with State Route 24, near the western boundary of Capitol Reef National Park. Park visitation now totals more than 40,000 people annually, a number that doubtless will increase as these spectacular scenic routes become better known. For many visitors, the park's thirty-acre lake, Wide Hollow Reservoir, is reason enough for going there, especially during the summer when its elevation more than a mile above sea level offers welcome relief from valley heat. The lake offers boating, water sports, swimming, and fishing from spring to late fall, and ice fishing in winter. It is backed up behind a dam fifty feet high that was constructed in 1954 by a local irrigation cooperative. The lake has a storage capacity of 2,324 acre-feet of water and provides a dependable source of water for the arid Escalante Valley.

Two self-guiding nature trails, each about a mile and half long, lead to the park's more accessible areas where the petrified material may be seen (but not collected). Samples are on sale in Escalante and elsewhere in the region. Tons of the material were hauled away before the park was established, to be sold as souvenirs or for decorating fireplaces and rock gardens, among other misguided uses.

Escalante State Park, the town of Escalante, and the nearby Escalante River are named for a man who never came within seventy miles of any of them—Fray Silvestre Vélez de Escalante, a Spanish explorer-priest who wandered over much of what is now Utah in 1776. (*See* Green River and Starvation state parks for more about the Dominguez-Escalante expedition.)

It was a member of the John Wesley Powell survey party of 1872, one Almon Harris Thompson, who first explored the river and named it for Escalante. He later suggested to some Mormon settlers from Panguitch that they echo the name in their settlement, which they did when they platted a townsite in 1876 near the junction of Pine Creek and the river. The valley had been known as Potato Valley, from the edible wild tubers noted there by an earlier expedition.

Said to be the last important river discovered in the lower forty-eight states, the Escalante has been inventoried by the Department of the Interior as a potential national Wild and Scenic River, but to date (1988) no action has been taken by Congress to that end. The river flows ninety miles southeast to empty into Lake Powell, and it is sometimes navigable by expert river runners in kayaks or canoes during the spring runoff. It is, however, too risky for novices.

It was in the canyons of the Escalante that one of Utah's most mysterious figures disappeared in 1934. Then twenty years old, Everett Ruess was a dreamy wanderer from California who left behind letters, woodblock prints, and sketches of the canyon country that he explored on foot and with burros. His remains were never found, and mystery still shrouds his disappearance.

Now about the origins of the petrified wood. According to current theory, all of the petrified logs in the region are the remains of trees that were buried under accumulated sediments

along with fragments of dinosaur bones. The trees had been
stripped of their branches when rolled downstream in floods.
Shielded from oxygen and decay by the deep layers of silt, sand,
and gravel, the wood and bone were replaced, cell by cell, by
crystals of silicon dioxide, a process that took millions of years.
Later upheavals of the earth's crust cracked the logs into irregular
sections and scattered the buried bones. The breakage of the logs
was further advanced by the alternate freezing and thawing of
water that had seeped into the cracks.

Chemical impurities other than the white silicon dioxide
account for the rainbow colors. The reds, browns, and yellows
result primarily from iron compounds. Manganese and other
minerals account for the purples and dark blues of agate and
jasper, some of gem quality.

In addition to preserving the petrified materials, establishment
of the state park has afforded some protection for the numerous
Indian ruins, artifacts, and petroglyphs in the area, most of them
dating back centuries.

At the dedication of Fort Buenaventura State Park, October 30, 1980. Photograph by Vickie Bump, a Communications Services photo courtesy Utah State Division of Parks and Recreation.

60

Fort Buenaventura State Park

Open April-November
Picnicing
Museum
Replica of mountain man fort; stockade, cabins, mountain men activities.

Drinking water
Modern restrooms, wheelchair
    accessible

A replica of a mid-nineteenth-century trading post and compound, Fort Buenaventura State Park occupies sixty-eight acres along the Weber River near the center of Ogden, Utah's third-largest city. It is the site of the first Euro-American settlement in the Great Basin in the 1840s, at the close of the era of western exploration and fur trapping.

Open from April to November during daylight hours, the park has modern restroom facilities and a large paved parking area. The entrance is reached by taking the 31st Street exit from Interstate 15 northbound (southbound travelers should take the 24th Street exit), then turning east and following signs to the park.

The reconstructed fort was partly burned by vandals in the winter of 1982-83. Since then the park's stockade was rebuilt and a pioneer cabin added at a cost of more than $300,000. All construction details follow documented facts about forts of the period, so the replica is built entirely without nails, and wooden pegs and mortise-and-tenon joints hold the cottonwood logs together. The original Miles Goodyear pioneer cabin that occupied the site is still standing on Washington Boulevard between 21st and 22nd Streets next to the Mormon Tabernacle, where it was moved in 1928, and is protected by a canopy.

Members of an organization known as the Mountain Men hold a rendezvous at the park annually, living in tents or trailers, cooking over open fires, and conducting shooting contests with their muzzle-loading black-powder rifles, along with other activities. The rendezvous attracts large crowds of participants and spectators.

Fur trappers, including Peter Skene Ogden (1794-1854), an expedition leader for the Hudson's Bay Company for whom the city of Ogden later was named, visited the area as early as 1825. The first settler was Yankee trapper and trader Miles Goodyear, who brought his Ute Indian wife, Pomona, and two children to the site about 1845, built his cabin of cottonwood logs, and eventually established a trading post. The fur trade had ended when silk replaced beaver pelts in the manufacture of men's fashionable top hats, and Goodyear reckoned—wrongly, as it turned out—that a major route to the West Coast soon would be established through the area.

To his original cabin Goodyear added quarters for his partners and their families, and he enclosed the compound with a stockade of tall cottonwood poles. There is still some dispute about the actual date of Goodyear's arrival, which may have been any time between 1844 and 1847. State park literature fixes the date at 1846.

Goodyear had first come west as a youth from his native Connecticut, meeting up with the Oregon-bound Marcus Whitman party of 1836 and accompanying them as far as Fort Hall, Idaho. When the Whitman party moved on, Goodyear remained in the area, learning to hunt, trap, and trade until he struck out on his own. The trading post and fort he established on the Weber River was the first non-Indian settlement anywhere in the Great Basin.

The venture was rather short-lived. When the Mormons arrived in 1847 to start building Salt Lake City less than forty miles away, Goodyear found he had more company than he wanted. Further, church authorities feared that Goodyear's post might become a haven for dissatisfied members fleeing the infant settlement. Goodyear had dubious titles to the land he occupied, including much of what is now Ogden, but rather than getting involved in a protracted dispute, the church authorities paid Goodyear $1,950 for a quitclaim deed, and he left for California in 1848. Goodyear visited Fort Buenaventura briefly in July of 1849. He had bought a large herd of horses in California and had driven them east to St. Joseph, Missouri. Finding the market there unfavorable, he turned around and drove the herd all the way back (stopping in Utah on the way) to California. He arrived there in the summer of 1849, just in time for the Gold Rush, and made a huge profit. Horses were greatly in demand not only for transport but as a source of power—and meat—at the mines. Hungry miners were not finicky about their diet. There are few ventures in the annals of the Far West more dramatic than Goodyear's 4,000-mile round trip with a herd of horses braving deserts, lofty mountains, and hostile Indians. Goodyear died in California later the same year at a mine he and his brother Andrew were operating on the North Yuba River. The hamlet of Goodyear's Bar in the Sierra Nevada foothills is named for him. Andrew stashed his brother's remains in a coffin made from gold rockers until he could take the bones to Benecia, on upper San Francisco Bay, for a decent burial.

After Goodyear sold out to the church, the little settlement became known as Brownsville for a Captain James Brown of the Mormon Battalion who was sent there by Brigham Young to establish a community. With his five sons, Brown raised wheat and corn from seeds purchased in California, the only source of seeds at the time. The butter and cheese he made from the milk of cows and goats developed into Ogden's first industry.

The name Fort Buenaventura used by Goodyear recalled the name of a mythical river that explorers from earliest Spanish times had supposed would flow west into San Francisco Bay to provide easy access to the Pacific Ocean. Buenaventura, Spanish for good fortune or good journey, also was an early name applied to the Green River and some other streams that had not yet been fully explored. The assumption that river travel from the interior to the West Coast was possible represents a phenomenon called "the geography of hope" by Bernard DeVoto (1897–1955), Ogden-born writer, editor, and literary critic. He explained that when the world still depended largely upon water transportation, before railroads and automobiles, hope and wishful thinking played a major role in men's travel decisions. There simply *had* to be a navigable river running to the West Coast, so therefore there *was* one—only it did not exist. Even though a group of fur trappers circumnavigated the Great Salt Lake in skin boats or canoes in 1826—finding, of course, no outlet—it was not until John C. Frémont explored from the Great Salt Lake to the Sierras in 1843–44 that the myth of the river was finally put to rest. Frémont, in fact, coined the term "the Great Basin." The name Buenaventura survived only at Goodyear's outpost, was lost for more than a century after the Mormons took over, and was revived when the state park was created in 1979.

Figure inscribed on a cliff face at Fremont Indian State Park.

64

Fremont Indian State Park

Open all year
Day-use only
Picnicing
Visitor center/museum
Drinking water

Modern restrooms, wheelchair
    accessible
Fishing
Concessionaire

Museum featuring the Fremont Indian culture; rock art; interpretive trails; horseback riding.

Months before its strikingly handsome museum-visitor center and its interpretive trails were completed in mid-1987, Fremont Indian State Park's unusual displays of prehistoric dwellings, rock art, and artifacts were attracting hundreds of weekend and holiday visitors. The scarcity of highway signs indicating the park's access road on old State Route 4, just off Interstate 70 between Sevier Junction and Interstate 15, was no deterrent to enthusiasts from many states. Prehistoric relics that somehow escaped the ravages of time and vandals seem to hold a universal appeal for everyone.

Now marked with better signs, the day-use-only park discloses much hitherto little-known information about the ancient Fremont people for whom the park is named. In fact, the new museum is already an important repository of tangible artifacts relating to this obscure people, who vanished from the scene six or seven centuries ago.

Archaeologists think that the Fremont people, who were named for the river near which traces of them were first found in central Utah, were related to other desert-dwelling groups such as the Anasazi to the south (*see* Anasazi State Park). The Anasazi are known for their elaborate cliff and mesa-top house clusters in the Four Corners region (*see* Edge of the Cedars and Monument Valley state parks). The Fremont culture is notable for its unusual petroglyphs and pictographs, for its many unfired clay figurines, and for its unpainted gray ceramic ware, as well as for an unusual style of moccasin fashioned from the skins of animals. Some life-size humanoid rock paintings in Canyonlands National Park are ascribed by some archaeologists to the Fremont people,

David Magleby with his father, Marvin Magleby, at the 1987 dedication of Fremont Indian State Park. Ken Kohler photo.

although there is no direct evidence of their ever having settled there.

Whoever and whatever the Fremont people may have been, their extensive primitive dwellings along Clear Creek remained officially unknown until November 1983. When archaeological teams from Brigham Young University at Provo started an exploratory excavation in Clear Creek Canyon in advance of the extension of Interstate 70, the Sevier schools bussed several hundred students to view the project.

One third-grade student told the archaeologists that his father knew of a much better site nearby. The next morning the boy's father led them to Five Finger Knoll where his Sunday school teacher had taken his class some twenty-five years earlier. The boy and his father later attended the dedication ceremonies and were photographed with the Five Finger Knoll looming up behind them (*see* photo). Work on the highway extension was stopped until the archaeologists could excavate and record their findings in detail. Uncovered at the site were more than one hundred prehistoric pit houses (a type of primitive habitation made by surrounding a hole in the ground with timbers or slabs and roofing it over with brush and sod), along with a treasure trove of artifacts. The discovery led to the organization of the Clear Creek Archaeological Association, whose members successfully lobbied the state legislature for funds to carry on the salvage work and for state park status for the site. A $500,000 contract with Brigham Young University resulted in the recovery of thousands of artifacts; carbon dating of pieces of burned timber established that the site may have been occupied from A.D. 400 to 1300.

These resourceful, late Stone Age people appear to have cultivated corn, beans, and squash to supplement their diet on piñon nuts, acorns, wild seeds, bulbs, and berries. They hunted and snared small animals, caught fish in Clear Creek, and employed bows and arrows and throwing spears to take deer. In the state park museum large picture panels and a video program illustrate many of these activities. The Fremont people also found time to inscribe cliff faces with both pictographs (painted) and petroglyphs (incised), most of which are beyond interpretation for modern folks (see Newspaper Rock State Park). Reproductions of some of the figures are on display in the park museum.

Some of the artifacts would seem to indicate that Clear Creek Canyon was used for centuries as a trade route between Sevier Canyon and the Mineral Mountains (west of Interstate 15), where there are large deposits of obsidian. The black volcanic glass was chipped and flaked to make spear points, arrowheads, knives, and scrapers. Early Spanish and American trappers and explorers also traversed the route.

The discovery of gold in the 1890s high in the Tushar Mountains south of Clear Creek led to the boom-and-bust settlement of Kimberly, a small mining community. It flourished for about four decades with a steam power plant, a livery stable, a boarding house, and a one-room schoolhouse. Abandoned after 1938 when the gold mines petered out, it has now nearly vanished.

Sandstone turrets like huge chess pieces greet guests at entrance to Goblin Valley State Park.

Goblin Valley State Park

Open all year
Camping, 21 units
Picnicing
Drinking water
Modern restrooms, wheelchair accessible

Vault toilets
Showers
Sewage disposal
Off-highway vehicles, nearby

Intricately eroded rock formations; photography; hiking; exploring.

All things considered, Goblin Valley probably is as apt a name as the English language can offer for this extraordinary state park in the uninhabited San Rafael Desert between Green River and Hanksville, south of Interstate 70.

As the name may suggest, the park is unique, quite unlike any other state park in Utah, perhaps unlike any other place in the nation or anywhere else—short of the moon. To some visitors, the terrain resembles photos of the moon's surface; to others it is a phantasmagoria in petrified mud. Many find it downright spooky but at the same time awesome and strangely beautiful.

Artists and photographers especially should come prepared to stay a while, and they should bring with them ample supplies of the materials of their craft. The incredible scene awaiting them changes by the hour, the day, the time of year, with the weather, and with every fresh angle of view. Doubtless no two observers ever see the same things.

In more precise terms, the valley is a long, narrow trough in the southeastern quarter of the great, ancient rock formation known as the San Rafael Reef, the east face of the canyon-cleft San Rafael Swell. At Goblin Valley, colorful eroded cliffs enclose untold thousands of grotesque forms sculpted in a deep layer of solidified mud deposited by primordial seas anywhere from 140 to 200 million years ago. Save for a lack of anything to eat, dinosaurs would appear to be quite at home here.

The carving process that has produced all those weird forms continues apace, carried on by millennia of wind and rain. The process is often visible as the nearly constant wind gnaws away at the chocolate-colored rocks and blows sand into the observer's eyes, food, and cameras.

The shapes that result from all this action do look like goblins, to be sure, or like the comic-strip shmoos; some resemble mudheads, the ceremonial clowns of the Zuni Indians. A few visitors see the shapes as dancers, as they appear to move with the wind through the stately steps of a minuet; others regard them as members of a vast herd of sea animals trapped when the waters vanished. Their resemblance to sea lions or walrus is astonishing, for all their lack of sounds or smells.

It seems little short of a miracle that the valley remained undiscovered and thus unexploited until it could be rescued and preserved. It was virtually unknown except for an occasional cowhand hunting lost livestock until 1949, when it was explored and photographed by a party led by Arthur Chaffin, a prominent figure in the Southwest who was a promoter of Utah's scenic wonders, owner-operator of the old Hite ferry on the Colorado River, and a Wayne County commissioner. Actually, Chaffin had stumbled across the valley some twenty years earlier while searching on horseback for a feasible route for an oil company road between Green River and Caineville. His second exploration brought what he had called "Mushroom Valley" to public attention. It was proposed as a national park, but instead was acquired by the state as a reserve in 1954. The state paid $5,600 for 2,240 acres, then leased another thousand acres or so from the Bureau of Land Management in 1984. The park now encompasses 3,254 acres, five square miles almost exactly a mile above sea level. At the end of a graded road past the campground, a covered observation station and picnic area overlook part of the valley, and a foot trail winds through the odd crowds of mud figures. The road can be somewhat slippery in wet weather.

While vegetation is generally sparse except for a planted area around the ranger station, typical desert growth may be found here and there including saltbush, rabbit brush, Mormon tea, wild buckwheat, lupine, several kinds of cactus, locoweed, vetch, Indian rice grass, and snakeweed.

Most of the surprisingly varied wildlife is nocturnal and therefore seldom seen, but it is not safe to leave food out in the open for pack rats to feast upon. Believe it or not, mule deer and pronghorn antelope inhabit the area, along with skunks, porcupines, kangaroo rats, kit foxes, coyotes, bobcats, jackrabbits, badgers, and gophers, not to mention numerous collared lizards and chuckwallas, a few scorpions, and perhaps an occasional rattlesnake.

As well named as Goblin Valley, Temple Mountain stands like a cathedral above the San Rafael Reef a few miles north of the park. During the uranium rush of the 1950s the mountain was extensively explored, and many tunnels and pits remain as hazards for the unwary hiker. (Old mines are inviting, but hikers should never explore them. Several people have died in old mines in recent years. The state is in the process of sealing up many old sites, but funds are limited and progress slow.)

The main access road leading to the mine area is paved part of the way, threading through a narrow canyon where some prehistoric Indian petroglyphs may be seen. The road continues northward to intersect Interstate 70 some thirty miles west of Green River. The wild back country is popular with the ATV (all-terrain vehicle) set, who use the park as a rallying point.

This road and many others from the uranium boom lace a fascinating upwelling of bare rock and sheer cliffs, the San Rafael Swell. Popular with hikers, backpackers, and wanderers, the Swell's dozens of canyons have waterfalls, Indian ruins, tiny oases made by canyon springs, the rare desert bighorn sheep, and marvelous, surprising rock formations. Sometimes referred to as "Utah's sixth national park" (along with Zion, Bryce Canyon, Capitol Reef, Arches, and Canyonlands), the Swell *has* been proposed for designation as a national park, or—failing that—a national conservation area under the jurisdiction of the Bureau of Land Management. Opponents want to keep the area open to cattle grazing, oil and gas leases, and ATV riding.

Tiny dots on river's edge at extreme lower left of photo are rafts going down the San Juan River as seen from overlook at Goosenecks of the San Juan State Park.

Goosenecks of the San Juan State Park

Open all year   Picnicing
Camping, 3 units   Drinking water
Group camping   Off-highway vehicles, nearby
1,000-foot-deep chasm carved by the San Juan River; panoramic overlook; photography.

One of these days, give or take a few million years, the silt-laden San Juan River in southeastern Utah is likely to convert some of the towering vertical cliffs that line it into a series of natural bridges. That will be quite a sight, perhaps one of the world's great scenic wonders, even if there are no tourists around to be awestruck by the spectacle.

But today, even without natural bridges, the great Goosenecks of the San Juan, viewed from the overlook at the state park, are awesome to most, puzzling to many. An informational signboard tells the story in brief:

"Geologists consider this part of the river to be one of the finest examples of 'entrenched meanders' anywhere in the world.

"The meandering pattern originated several million years ago when the river was flowing on a relatively flat plain, much as the present-day Mississippi River.

"The San Juan became entrenched when the entire Colorado Plateau was slowly uplifted. Cutting downward, the river followed its initial pattern and thus created the canyon you now view.

"The process continues to this day as the San Juan River cuts ever deeper into prehistoric geological formations."

What the signboard does not say is that some of the loops and bends in the river's course, called oxbows or horseshoe bends, have undercut their walls almost to the point of tunneling through. One large meander visible from the park's overlook has a neck less than 100 yards wide, although the loop the river follows is three miles around.

The little ten-acre state park is reached by a paved road (State Routes 261 and 316) off U.S. Highway 163 four miles north of the town of Mexican Hat on the San Juan River. Open all year, the park has minimal facilities—a small parking area, a covered observation shelter, a few primitive campsites, and some pit toilets. There is no water or firewood. Native American vendors are often seen at the site selling jewelry, beaded goods, rugs, and other wares.

Because of the aridity of the region around Goosenecks of the San Juan State Park, wildlife is scarce—mainly rabbits, rodents, the usual desert reptiles, an occasional fox, bobcat, or coyote. Migratory birds follow the course of the river. Golden eagles, red-tailed hawks, ravens, and cliff swallows soar overhead but seldom are plentiful.

Vegetation is typical of the high deserts of the Southwest, including the ubiquitous sagebrush, saltbush, and blackbrush, as well as prickly pear, Russian thistle, Indian ricegrass, and various ephemeral wildflowers dependent upon the unpredictable rainfall. Most of the rainfall is likely (but not certain) to come in summer storms that may produce flash floods. Winter and spring usually are relatively dry save for snow now and then, rarely heavy enough to impair travel. Summer temperatures at ground level often exceed a very dry 100 degrees; winter lows can dip well below freezing.

As one disenchanted cowboy is quoted as saying of the plateau country, "There's plenty of room to swing a cow by the tail, but hardly enough grass to feed one." Perhaps that is why the federal Bureau of Land Management, often more interested in grazing than in scenic grandeur, sold the ten-acre park site to the state for $50 in 1962.

Not all of the 40,000 to 50,000 visitors estimated to visit the park every year see it from the end of the entrance road. Numbers of adventurers follow the river's meanders in kayaks or rafts, visible from the overlook as ant-size Lilliputians taking the long way around the bends.

An even more spectacular view of the San Juan's great meanders may be had from Muley Point Overlook outside the state park (follow State Route 261 nine miles north to the turnoff). Since it is nearly a thousand feet higher than the state park, Muley Point encompasses an even broader panorama, including some of the distant buttes and pinnacles of Monument Valley. State Route 261 continues due north to State Route 95 (the Bicentennial Highway) near Natural Bridges National Monument. State Route 95 crosses further west the upper reaches of Lake Powell at Hite Marina.

For an extremely interesting alternative route, take 261 to 95, then turn south off 95 onto State Route 276 seven miles west of Natural Bridges and follow it down to Lake Powell at Hall's Crossing. Along with Lee's Ferry in Arizona and Dandy Crossing to the north near Hite, it was one of three places where the river could be readily crossed before it became a lake.

Now a large motor ferry carries passengers and vehicles from Hall's Crossing to Bullfrog Basin, whence State Route 276 loops back to State Route 95 west of Hite. The ferry is called *John Atlantic Burr*, named for a pioneer Utah rancher of the region. The Burr Trail, a primitive road running from the east side of the Waterpocket Fold to Boulder (*see* Anasazi State Park) also is named for him.

The ferry is a steel craft built for the purpose in Salt Lake City. Powered by two big diesel engines, it is 100 feet long and 42 feet wide. It has a capacity of eight automobiles and two buses, with a maximum passenger load of 150. The craft's construction was funded by the Utah Department of Transportation. It makes a round trip every two hours, leaving Hall's Crossing on even numbered hours, Bullfrog on the odd. From May 15 to September 30, it runs from 8 A.M. to 7 P.M.; the rest of the year 8 A.M. to 3 P.M. The crossing, a distance of three miles, takes about twenty minutes. All trips are subject to cancellation or postponement in foul weather.

Flooded pavilion and yacht harbor at Saltair Beach.

76

Great Salt Lake State Park

Open all year	Showers
Day-use only	Sewage disposal
Picnicing	Boating
Visitor center/museum	Swimming
Drinking water	Concessionaire
Modern restrooms	

America's inland sea; salt water bathing; sailing; photography.

To attempt to tell here the full story of Saltair Beach on the south shore and its many historic counterparts along the Great Salt Lake's south and east shores would be both futile and presumptuous.

It would be futile because the beaches change continually as the level of the lake water fluctuates. It would be presumptuous because the 150-year history of the beaches and their sometimes palatial resorts is the history of the lake itself, which has been the subject of works already filling library shelves.

Perhaps the simplest way to explain the current situation is to offer some numbers. The official state park brochure, published in 1983, indicated that the level of the lake was just about 4,200 feet above sea level. By 1987 the lake had risen to the unprecedented level of 4,212 feet above mean sea level, give or take an inch or so. But such an increase in the lake's level can cover thousands of acres of the flatlands surrounding the lake with disastrous flooding the result. To combat the lake's relentless rise, the state started a huge pumping scheme in 1987 (*see* Antelope Island State Park).

The flooding has meant, among other things, that by 1987 once glamorous Saltair Beach lay beneath eight or ten feet of salt water. To accommodate the great hordes of residents and visitors who regard the lake as a vast playground, a place where one could "float like a cork" while getting sunburned, some primitive facilities were installed along a four-mile stretch of artificial beach just above the last high-water mark. By ordinary standards, amenities were seriously lacking, but still there was hardly standing room on any sunny weekend.

Building sand castles on Saltair Beach.

The beach (in late 1988) was a long, narrow strip running along the lake from the junction of Interstate 80 with State Route 202 (sixteen miles west of downtown Salt Lake City), to a boat harbor and a modern mini-replica of the old Moorish-style Saltair Pavilion where generations of Utahns swam, boated, and danced. The new Saltair, too, was flooded in the mid-1980s. The first Saltair was largely a project of the Mormon Church to provide wholesome recreation for its members. Built in 1893 on 2,500 pilings driven into the lake bottom, the structure had a vaguely Middle Eastern look, with a dome 100 feet high, mosquelike towers, and a grandly arched entrance. Refreshment stands, bathhouses, and "the world's largest outdoor dance floor" provided for the needs of thousands. Saltair declined in popularity after World War II and was destroyed by fire in 1970. (For more on the history of this resort see Nancy D. and John S. McCormick's *Saltair* and Dale Morgan's classic *The Great Salt Lake*.)

The yacht harbor, which provides mooring for some 300 sailing craft, is not far from Lake Point, once the westernmost of the famous old lakeside resorts. Now there is no trace of the many elaborate pleasure palaces and multi-million-dollar resorts that formerly dotted the lakeshore from Lake Point all the way to Syracuse, just outside Ogden.

What happened to all those resorts and pavilions, all the roller coasters and honky-tonks, all the hot-dog stands and fancy eateries? They burned down, or were flooded when the lake rose, or were left high and dry when the lake went down again in its usual yo-yo fashion. Prior to the 1920s, and for a little while thereafter, people went to the beaches and their glamorous adjuncts mostly by train, by horse and buggy, even by lake steamer. Then modern automobiles and paved highways took over and too many of the pleasure seekers went elsewhere.

To date, no modern-day Kubla Khan has appeared on the scene to decree any more stately pleasure domes at Great Salt Lake's Xanadu. To build on the shores of the Great Salt Lake requires a crystal ball to outguess its fickle and wholly unpredictable fluctuations.

At a rest stop somewhere on the Green River below Green River State Park. State Park photo by Norman Van Pelt.

80

Green River State Park

Open all year	Showers
Camping, 42 units	Sewage disposal
Picnicing	Boating/fishing
Drinking water	Off-highway vehicles, nearby
Modern restrooms, wheelchair accessible	

Major overnight camping spot; embarkation point for river float trips.

A pleasant surprise in its own right, Green River State Park's location suggests its strategic importance and accounts, at least in part, for its annual visitor total of more than 100,000.

Situated in the century-old town of Green River, the park's well-kept grounds, shaded by dozens of large cottonwood trees, appear as a welcome oasis in the seemingly endless rocky desert east and west along Interstate 70. The park lies at the only vehicle crossing of the Green River in a stretch of nearly 300 miles.

North of the town, the big river winds and twists some ninety-five miles through spectacular Desolation and Gray Canyons, popular with river runners, most of whom leave the river at the park. The park's paved boat ramp is also much used by downriver expeditions taking advantage of the ensuing 118 miles of relatively smooth water before the Green joins the Colorado. Others, more ambitious, continue on down through the wild rapids of Cataract Canyon to Lake Powell, or turn left at the confluence of the Green and the Colorado in Canyonlands National Park to buck the surging river in powerboats back up to Moab, fifty miles to the southeast of Green River.

In addition to its boating facilities, the park offers forty-two developed campsites, piped water, lighted and heated restrooms with showers (warmly welcomed by weary travelers), and small amphitheater where interpretive programs are presented during the busy summer season. A museum for the park is in the planning stage.

The riverside location of the park attracts much wildlife, including resident robins, kingbirds, mourning doves, and egrets, herons, hawks, owls, and sundry warblers. Beavers and muskrats

Entrance station, Green River State Park.

inhabit the riverbanks and may be seen swimming in the river at daybreak and at dusk, while squirrels romp through the trees and catfish and carp splash the river's surface.

For more than twenty years the park has been the starting place for the widely celebrated Memorial Day weekend Friendship Cruise, which has attracted hundreds of powerboats in the past. Originally conceived as a race, the event soon became a well-organized regatta drawing participants from all over the country. Dwindling participation, however, has cast the future of the cruise in doubt.

The idea of a Memorial Day powerboat race was cooked up at a Green River Chamber of Commerce meeting in the winter of 1957-58, and the Moab Chamber of Commerce enthusiastically joined in. As a publicity stunt, members of the press were invited to go on a preliminary river trip. This proved to be so popular that a flotilla of thirty boats had to be organized just to carry the newspaper people.

By 1960, the race had burgeoned into the Friendship Cruise, a gala social event that sometimes lasted three days. A shuttle service was set up to move vehicles and boat trailers from Green River to Moab, and fuel depots were established at various points along the river. The town and the state park still sponsor an annual canoe trip that runs seventy miles down the river to a place called Mineral Bottoms on the north boundary of Canyonlands National Park, from where a primitive dirt road leads back toward Moab.

But even without the Friendship Cruise and river trips, Green River has long been a center for tourist activity, situated as it is on a major transcontinental highway within a two-hour drive of Goblin Valley, Dead Horse Point, Huntington, Millsite, and Scofield Lake state parks; Arches, Canyonlands, and Capitol Reef national parks; the vast Lake Powell National Recreation Area; three national forests; and two Bureau of Land Management recreation sites.

Green River was a busy place off and on between 1963 and 1979 aside from the highway and river traffic. During that time the army launched many big Pershing and Athena land-to-land guided missiles from a site southeast of town. The missiles impacted on the White Sands Missile Range in southern New Mexico. The Green River operation employed hundreds of officers, enlisted men, and civilian workers.

Many varieties of trees give welcome shade at Green River State Park.

The town of Green River dates from about 1876, when a man named Blake won a contract to deliver the U.S. mail by packtrain from La Sal, south of Moab, to Salina, far to the west. Soon a small community grew up beside Blake's mail station at the Green River crossing (there was no bridge then). When the Denver and Rio Grande Western Railroad completed its route across Utah in 1883 (the last spike was driven a few miles west), its station was named Green River. The postmaster, one J. T. Farrer, asked the Post Office Department to change the name of his post office to Green River to coincide with the railroad station but the name remained Blake for some time.

Probably because of confusion with Green River, Wyoming, which had been founded much earlier, the name was changed on December 5, 1895, to one word, Greenriver, but in 1951 it became, once again, two words. (In case you were wondering, the "Green River Ordinance," prohibiting door-to-door peddling in the day-time, originated in the Wyoming, not the Utah, town as a boon to day-sleeping railroad crews stopping there.)

Some accounts still confuse the river crossing at the town of Green River with another one called Gunnison's Crossing, a wide ford about twenty miles north on the Old Spanish Trail. There Captain John W. Gunnison of the U.S. Army's Corps of Topo-graphical Engineers forded the river in 1853 with a pack train and a military escort. He was searching for a feasible route for a projected transcontinental railroad approaching from the east.

A month later, Gunnison and several members of his party were ambushed and killed by Pavant Indians near present-day Delta in western Utah. The action was thought to have been in reprisal for the wanton slaying of an elderly Pavant chieftain by a member of an emigrant party that had recently passed through the region. Gunnison Butte on the river a little north of Green River was named for him, as were a river, a mountain, a town, a county, a tunnel, and an island in the Great Salt Lake.

As for the east-west highway route through the town: when Interstate 70 was opened to traffic late in 1970, the portion west of Green River was proclaimed by the State Department of Transportation to be the "longest stretch of new interstate highway through previously untouched territory to be opened in this century." The new route crosses the forbidding rock-bound wilderness known as the San Rafael Swell (*see* Goblin Valley State Park), little known to the traveling public and still largely unexplored except by prospectors and off-road-vehicle fanatics.

The Naming and Taming of the Green

Watching the wide river's silt-laden slurry flowing past Green River State Park, one might well wonder how it came to be known by a name so suggestive of limpid pools and sylvan delights. The answer dates back to earliest Spanish times and involves one of the most turbulent chapters in the history of the western frontier—that wild scramble for beaver pelts to make high-crowned hats for men of fashion in the late eighteenth and first half of the nineteenth centuries.

The beaver trade was directly responsible for much of the early exploration of the Mountain West and the naming of its streams all the way to their alpine sources. That was long before anyone knew how the rivers reached the sea—if, indeed, they did. Quite aptly, the beaver has been called "the rodent that won the West."

Although the Green River's name almost certainly is a translation of the Spanish "Rio Verde," the name—like much else in the region—is often associated with General William Ashley. He was, among other things, the Missouri entrepreneur who organized the first large-scale rendezvous of beaver trappers in southern Wyoming and northern Utah in the mid-1820s. The upper part of the Green originally was known to frontiersmen by its Indian name, the Seedskadee (meaning prairie hen), spelled phonetically in many different ways.

The Spanish explorers Dominguez and Escalante, who in 1776 crossed the river and camped beside it a little way north of present-day Jensen, Utah, called it the Rio San Buenaventura. Since they had only a hazy idea of where they were at the time, they had no notion at all as to where the river came from or where it was going. Nor could they have known that they probably were the first non-Indians ever to see it.

Later, various parts of the river were called by other names, including the Spanish River, the Rio del Norte or North River, and the Colorado of the West. Some accounts of early trappers and explorers confused the Green with what is now called the Colorado, often referring to the section of the Colorado above its junction with the Green as Grand River. Some thought they were

86

separate rivers emptying into the Pacific Ocean somewhere along the California coast.

Nobody then seemed to realize that the Green was in fact a great river in its own right, flowing through 291 miles in what was to become Wyoming, forty-two miles in Colorado, and 397 in Utah before joining the Colorado in what is now Canyonlands National Park.

At any rate, Ashley and his mountain men eventually began calling this brawling, beaver-rich river the Green, in keeping with their penchant for short, descriptive, and no-nonsense names, such as Big Sandy and Henry's Fork. True origin of the Spanish name is not known for certain, but it probably referred to the cool green color of the unsullied water that contrasts so strongly with the muddy red of the Colorado. One historian suggested that the name derived from the color of soapstones that paved the river's bottom along one long stretch. Another asserted that Ashley named the river for one of his companions. Captain John C. Frémont, crossing the upper river in the mid-1840s on one of his tours of discovery, wrote in his diary that he thought the name was derived from the stream's timbered shores and green wooded islands, in contrast to the surrounding dry and sandy sagebrush plains. In any event, the name stuck.

Yet another use of the term "Green River" found its way into the vocabulary of the fur trappers in the form of a knife manufactured in Green River, Massachusetts, and sold by the thousands to the fur trade. It was a handy culinary tool, as useful for carving buffalo meat as it was for skinning a beaver, but its name eventually acquired a more sinister meaning.

When a Green River knife was sunk to the hilt between the ribs of the loser in hand-to-hand combat, the lettering "Green River Works" on the blade near the handle was buried. Thus, to give an opponent "the works" meant (as it still does) that the blade had gone in all the way with fatal effect, that the work had been done "to the hilt." Or that's the story.

Incidentally, while seeking a water route to carry his bales of fur to market, Ashley himself made a pioneering junket in a bullboat down the river in the vicinity of Dinosaur National Monument on the border of Colorado. He turned back about twenty-four miles below the present-day town of Duchesne, after capsizing at least once, and went overland to meet the trappers at the first

rendezvous in southern Wyoming, having convinced himself that
the route was far too rough ever to serve any useful purpose. He
could not have dreamed that river running would become a major
recreational enterprise instead of a hazardous chore.

The Green River name was firmly established by the time
Major John Wesley Powell brought his intrepid if uneasy little
band of men and four clumsy wooden boats to the river at Green
River, Wyoming, in 1869. Powell did not change the name of the
river but he did give colorful and sometimes poetic names to many
of the landmarks along the Green and lower Colorado: Flaming
Gorge, Horseshoe Canyon, Kingfisher Creek, Beehive Point, Music
Temple, Tapestry Wall, and the Gates of Lodore.

Powell and most of his party finally made it all the way down
to what is now the headwaters of Lake Mead in Nevada, proving
that it could be done despite many grim judgments to the contrary.
Others followed, first a trickle and then a flood. Now every mile of
both the Green and the Colorado is mapped and named, and
anyone wishing to run the Grand Canyon has to sign up well in
advance and wait. The river is so popular that a quota system has
been established to apportion campsites and protect riverside
ecological systems.

Although his is the first confirmed successful journey through
the great canyons, Powell may not have been the first to attempt it.
Earlier, between 1831 and 1836, a trapper and trader named Denis
Julien carved his name and the date at several places on the rocky
canyon walls along both the Green and the Colorado, the last at
the lower end of Cataract Canyon. How he got that far and what
happened to him after that is another of the canyon's gloomy
secrets.

Gunlock State Park

Open all year   Boating/fishing
Camping   Swimming
Vault toilets
Scenic red rock country; year-round water sports; boating; fishing.

Even though the lake that is Gunlock State Park's only reason for existence did not appear until 1970, perhaps its most remarkable aspect is its name, which dates back more than a century in regional history. Oddly enough, the name Gunlock derives from the nickname of a frontiersman whose main claim to fame was that he was a brother of the renowned early-day Mormon settler and missionary, Jacob Hamblin.

In the extreme southwestern corner of the state, the lake has 266 acres of blue water that draw some 50,000 visitors a year from as far away as Cedar City and Las Vegas, despite an almost total lack of amenities usually found in state parks. Two miles long by half a mile wide, the lake has a maximum depth of 115 feet. It was created in 1969-70 by the construction of an earth-fill dam on the Santa Clara River by the Lower Gunlock Reservoir Corporation. Built primarily for irrigation and flood control purposes, the reservoir has a storage capacity of 11,000 acre feet of water behind a dam 117 feet high.

The lake is stocked by the Division of Wildlife Resources with largemouth bass, black crappie, threadfin shad, and channel catfish. Also present are some bluegill, green sunfish, and desert suckers. The division contributed to the cost of the dam in return for the right to maintain a minimum pool of 2,300 acre feet of stored water for fish culture and experimentation.

Gunlock Lake and the state park derive their name from the nearby hamlet of Gunlock, a tiny farming community a mile north of the lake on the road to Veyo. Gunlock has had a post office since 1883, serving a scattering of farms. It was named in honor of William Haynes (Gunlock Will or Bill) Hamblin, who was in his time a famous hunter and sharpshooter and a brother of Jacob Hamblin, pioneer missionary to the Indians of southern Utah and

Power boats and sailing craft share launching ramp at Gunlock State Park.

northern Arizona. Jacob was a particular friend of the Shivwits tribe of Paiute Indians, a handful of whose descendants still occupy a small reservation south of the lake on the road to Santa Clara.

William Hamblin, born in Ohio in 1830, settled on the Old Spanish Trail south of the present town of Gunlock in 1857. An elder in the Mormon church, he soon became well known for his skill in repairing gunlocks (the firing mechanism of firearms) and was called Gunlock Bill (or Will) the rest of his life. Twice married (to sisters), he fathered seventeen children. He died in Nevada in 1872 while on a trip in connection with a silver mine he had located near Pioche.

The original settlement was washed out in a flood in the winter of 1861-62. When it was rebuilt a mile upstream, the little community became known as Gunlock. The name gained official status when a U.S. post office was established there eleven years after Gunlock's death.

The county road that passes Gunlock Lake is a part of the Old Spanish Trail from Santa Fe, New Mexico, to Los Angeles. Passing through western Utah, it was used by raiders and horsemen from the 1820s until shorter routes to the California gold fields were developed after 1849. About fifteen miles to the north is the site of the Mountain Meadows Massacre, an infamous chapter in Mormon history. It was at the Mountain Meadows in 1857 that a mixed group of Mormon settlers and Paiute Indians murdered 120 men, women, and children from a wagon train bound for California. A monument near the highway marks the spot.

Busy campground scene in Huntington State Park.

Huntington State Park

Open all year
Camping, 22 units
Picnicing
Group pavilion
Drinking water
Modern restrooms, wheelchair accessible

Showers
Sewage disposal
Boating/fishing
Off-highway vehicles, nearby
Swimming

Scenic red rock country; year-round water sports; boating; fishing.

Huntington State Park's 111 acres of grass and planted trees beside a 129-acre lake give it the appearance of a city park, although it is situated in a semi-arid setting two miles from the nearest town and twenty-odd miles from a city of any size.

Near the town of Huntington on State Route 10, it is a convenient base for visits to numerous outdoor attractions in the area, including the Cleveland-Lloyd Dinosaur Quarry, several quaint old mining camps and ghost towns in the nearby foothills, and the many Forest Service campgrounds and fishing streams in the Manti-La Sal National Forest along State Route 31 west of the lake. Route 31 continues over the mountains to join U.S. Highway 89 at Fairview.

The Cleveland-Lloyd Dinosaur Quarry, eighteen miles east of Huntington on a gravel road, derives its name from the village of Cleveland and from Malcolm Lloyd, Jr., of Princeton University, who helped finance early excavations. Since the 1960s, thousands of fossil bones have been excavated there under the direction of the Bureau of Land Management and paleontologists from the University of Utah and the Utah Division of State History. The quarry is in a formation similar to that found at Dinosaur National Monument in northeastern Utah and dates back some 140 million years. Visitor accommodations include a picnic area and interpretive exhibits provided by the BLM and the Castle Valley Job Corps.

The lake and the state park are named for the town of Huntington, settled in 1877, which in turn was named for the three pioneer Huntington brothers—Oliver, Dimick, and William R.—

Inside the Bureau of Land Management visitor center at the Cleveland-Lloyd Dinosaur Quarry near Cleveland, Utah.

who first explored the region in 1855. Oliver was the official recorder for the unsuccessful Elk Mountain Mission to Moab, Dimick served as an interpreter to the local Indians, and William was famous as a scout and explorer.

Huntington North Reservoir, as the lake is officially designated, was constructed in 1965-66 by the U.S. Bureau of Reclamation for the Emery County Conservancy District. Its dam is 9,300 feet long and seventy-six feet high, containing a maximum of 5,600 acre feet of water for irrigation use in Castle Valley. A distribution reservoir for the Joe's Valley Project, it receives its water through a canal system from Joe's Valley and Huntington Creek.

Since 1969, the lake's recreation facilities have been developed and managed by the Utah State Division of Parks and Recreation under a lease agreement. Besides its camping and picnic facilities, the park is popular for its boating, fishing, and other water sports, as well as hiking, photography, bird watching, lawn games, and waterfowl hunting. In winter it serves as a base for snowmobiling and ice fishing.

Several small communities in the vicinity have interesting names and histories. Orangeville, a dozen miles to the south, was named for one Orange Seely, who settled there in 1875. Reputed to weigh more than 320 pounds, Seely nonetheless was able and willing to set out on horseback in any kind of weather to set broken bones or pull teeth whenever or wherever his services were needed. The town of Wellington, eight miles southeast of Price on U.S. Highway 6, was named for Orange's brother, Justus Wellington Seely.

The hamlet of Cleveland, seven miles to the east, dates from 1885 and was named for the sitting president, Grover Cleveland, who served two separate terms (1885-89 and 1893-97). Elmo, three miles north of Cleveland, at first was supposedly called Carson after Kit Carson, but the settlers later decided to call the place St. Elmo, and then shortened it to Elmo. In turn, that name presumably was taken from the title of a book, *St. Elmo*, written by someone named John Fox, Jr.

Also in the vicinity are three coal mining camps named Mohrland, Hiawatha, and Wattis. Of the three, only Hiawatha is still an active community. With a population of 249 in the 1980 census, it is said to be one of Utah's best-preserved coal mining camps of World War I vintage.

Boats on the jewel-like lake at Hyrum State Park.

96

Hyrum State Park

Open April-November
Camping, 39 units
Group camping
Picnicing
Visitor center
Drinking water

Modern restrooms, wheelchair
 accessible
Vault toilets
Showers
Utility hookups
Boating/fishing
Swimming

457 surface-acre reservoir; boating; water activities; camping; year-round fishing.

Some 200,000 visitors per year come to play on the Hyrum Reservoir, a jewel-like lake in far northern Utah where a handful of trappers long ago hid a fortune in furs, thus giving the French-Canadian name "cache" to the valley and later to the county centered there. A historical signboard near Hyrum State Park's visitor center tells a bit of the saga of those hardy adventurers who preceded by a third of a century the pioneer Mormon settlers in the valley of the Little Bear River. Here, on the edge of what is now Hyrum Reservoir, General William H. Ashley's rugged crew supposedly cached an estimated $150,000 in furs, mostly beaver, in the winter of 1825-26. They stashed the baled furs in a cave they dug in a clay bank to be safe from animals, insects, Indians, and the weather, a common practice of the trade. When in the summer of 1826 the high passes over the Wasatch range had opened and overland travel was possible again, Ashley returned to retrieve his furs and transport them by pack train and river raft to St. Louis, a long and arduous undertaking in itself.

Long before Hyrum Reservoir was built, the early Mormon settlers had to dig nine miles of canal to bring irrigation water from the Little Bear River. Having only hand tools for the task, they devised what they called a "go-devil" to speed the work. It consisted of two split logs fastened together at one end to make a crude V-shaped plow pulled by oxen. This apparatus pushed the dirt aside and greatly assisted in the digging.

Hyrum Reservoir was created in 1939 to provide irrigation

97

The lake at Hyrum State Park.

water for the farms of the wide and fertile Cache Valley. Built by the U.S. Bureau of Reclamation, the dam is an earth-fill-and-concrete structure 540 feet long at the top and 116 feet high. When it is full, it backs up 18,000 acre feet of water with a surface area of 457 acres. In recent years the town of Hyrum — which is named for Hyrum Smith, brother of the founder of the Mormon church — has expanded to include the area surrounding the lake, with some residences overlooking the 258-acre park.

In 1959 the Utah Division of Parks and Recreation took over administration of the lake for recreation purposes. In addition to picnic and camping facilities, the park has a boat dock and launching ramps and beaches for swimming. While the park is only open from April through November, during most winters the frozen lake is popular with ice fishermen and skaters. Shade trees, lawns, and flower gardens around the visitor center and at a newly developed day-use facility a mile east are among the park's summer attractions.

Hyrum State Park also serves as a convenient base camp for visitors to Blacksmith Fork Canyon on State Route 101 east of Hyrum. The stream is noted for its excellent brown trout fishing. Another unusual feature of the stream is a series of old beaver dams that have become so heavily coated with calcium carbonate (lime) from the stream's hard water that they appear to be solid rock.

At Hardware Ranch seventeen miles up Blacksmith Fork Canyon, large herds of elk are fed every winter, usually between December and March when winter snows cover their natural forage. The winter feeding is carried out by the state's Division of Wildlife Resources, which owns the ranch and maintains it for that purpose. Visitors are transported on horse-drawn sleighs that weave in and out among the hundreds of wintering elk.

Stagecoach with plastic passenger at Iron Mission State Park.

100

Iron Mission State Park

Open all year
Day-use only
Picnicing
Museum

Drinking water
Modern restrooms, wheelchair
    accessible
Off-highway vehicles, nearby

Pioneer museum; horse-drawn vehicles; pioneer and Indian artifacts.

Busy Cedar City, southern Utah's second largest city, sprawls beside Interstate 15, mecca for hordes of tourists.

To the pioneers who were sent there more than a century and a quarter ago to establish a colony and build an iron works, it must have seemed like the end of the world on the wild western frontier 300 wagon miles from Salt Lake City.

The story of that ill-fated outpost of the early 1850s is told in the varied exhibits at Iron Mission State Park in Cedar City, along with a display of Indian artifacts and old-time horse-drawn vehicles. The park's odd name reflects the reason for the pioneer settlement: large-scale iron deposits in the adjacent mountains, which resulted in the first iron foundry west of the Mississippi.

Until the transcontinental railroad arrived in Utah in 1869, iron for all kinds of domestic and industrial uses, from andirons to rims for wagon wheels, from nails to sleigh runners, was very hard to come by. After extensive iron deposits in what is now Iron County were discovered in 1849, President Brigham Young of the Mormon church called for volunteers to settle the region and to initiate a critically needed iron industry.

When the call failed to elicit much enthusiasm, the Mormon leader proclaimed the project to be a "work mission" and sent the first wave of colonists to set it up. The largest Mormon colonizing expedition up to that time, the party left Fort Utah in December 1850 in 129 wagons. The group consisted of 119 men, 31 women over fourteen years of age, and 18 children under fourteen. They took with them firearms, saddles, window glass, tools, seeds, saws, plows, scythes, and other farm implements, as well as cats, dogs, chickens, milk cows, beef cattle, oxen, mules, and horses.

Their first destination was to become the town of Parowan,

101

eighteen miles north of present-day Cedar City, where they wintered over and later in the spring planted crops to feed the colony. In the years following the Gold Rush of 1849, Parowan served as a supply base for the overland route from Salt Lake City to southern California.

Still the county seat of Iron County and known as the "Mother of the South," Parowan today is bypassed by the main highway. It is an attractive community of perhaps 2,000 residents, including some who commute to Cedar City. It has three old buildings listed in the National Register of Historic Places: a rock church built in 1862, the Jesse Smith home built in 1856-57, and a Mormon meetinghouse built during World War I.

Planting completed, the miners and iron workers in the group moved southwest to build an iron foundry, at first called the Pioneer Iron Mission. Most of them were converts to Mormonism from England, Wales, and Sweden who had previous experience in foundry work. By the fall of 1852 they had managed to produce a small quantity of iron which was made into horseshoe nails and one pair of andirons.

At first the new community was known as Coal Creek because a nearby stream passed through some coal beds which the colonists planned to use to fuel the foundry. The village became Cedar Fort in 1853 when work had to be suspended because of the threat of Indian attack, and the men turned to building fortifications and to laying in grain, hay, and wood for the winter. Later the name Cedar City came into common use, referring to the groves of cedars (junipers) in the region.

Floods, the uncertainty of water power, severe winter weather, a grasshopper plague that devastated farms supplying food to the colony, and the lack of suitable fuel (the local coal proved to be almost useless for smelting ore) combined to spell failure for the project. After eight years of grueling labor and the expenditure of nearly $150,000 in church funds, the iron works closed down late in 1858. Iron production by that time had resulted in little more than some kitchen utensils, wagon-wheel rims, and machine castings.

The colony dwindled rapidly, but some of the families remained to develop agriculture and stock raising, which continues to this day. In 1897 Southern Utah State College was established in Cedar City. A branch line of the Union Pacific Railroad arrived in

1923, followed by an influx of tourists as the scenic wonders of southern Utah became known. The designation of Mukuntuweep National Monument (later Zion National Park) in 1909, followed by Bryce Canyon (1923) and nearby Cedar Breaks National Monument (1933), put Cedar City on the map. It also became the termi- nus for tours that included the Grand Canyon in Arizona along with the Utah parks.

Iron Mission State Park on North Main Street in Cedar City is a museum complex devoted to the history of the region, with special emphasis on early-day transportation. The eleven-acre site displays a wide variety of pioneer buildings, wagons, machinery, and the like. Both inside and outside the main building are many examples of horse-drawn vehicles such as coaches, buggies, carts, surreys, and sleighs.

Most of the exhibits were collected and restored by the late Gronway Perry of Cedar City, a pioneer in the transportation industry who sold his collection to the city. A few years later, upon the establishment of the state park in 1973, the city donated the collection to the Division of Parks and Recreation.

A diorama based on written descriptions of the original iron foundry is among the historical exhibits which include dozens of antique tools, guns, churns, candle molds, saddles — even a bathtub and a wooden cigar-store Indian. The museum is open during daylight hours all year. A small admission fee is charged. Visitors total about 25,000 annually.

Cedar City was by no means the last or only place in the region where iron ore was mined and processed. The bright red-orange color of the surrounding hills indicates the presence of extensive iron deposits. The remains of a beehive charcoal oven and some ruins mark the site of Old Irontown, twenty-odd miles west off State Route 56. Irontown thrived during the 1870s and '80s, then faded into obscurity.

Closer to Cedar City, four or five miles to the northwest, Iron Springs and Desert Mound started production of iron ore in the 1920s, then burgeoned during World War II to reach a high point of four million tons as late as 1957. That output helped to feed the hungry furnaces in the giant Geneva steel plant at Orem, 250 miles to the north. Some of the first ore processed by the Iron Mission at Cedar City was dug there.

Peaceful scene along the Jordan River Parkway.

104

Jordan River State Park

Open all year
Day-use only
Picnicing
Group pavilion
Drinking water
Modern restrooms, wheelchair
  accessible
Vault toilets
Boating/fishing
Golfing

Riverside developments; jogging trail; canoeing; golf course; off-highway vehicle park; modelport.

Since the early 1970s more than $15 million has been invested in converting a noisome, polluted drain into the beginnings of a splendid recreational waterway. In prospect it promises to rival the older municipal river parkways of Denver, San Antonio, and Sacramento. Already canoeists and kayakers can float peacefully down the tree-shaded Jordan River for miles with little awareness of their urban surroundings.

It all started as an effort simply to improve the water quality of the river, which runs northward from Utah Lake to Great Salt Lake and for more than a century has served as a sewage and waste outlet for industries and communities all along the way. Another concern has been flood control, since the river has been known to increase its flow tenfold during spring runoff and to wreak havoc on farmlands, buildings, and roads along its meandering course.

As the State Department of Natural Resources reported in 1967, "What could be Utah's greatest asset has become its greatest liability, an open sewer unfit for aquatic life and recreation." At that time, industrial dumping alone was estimated to equal the raw sewage output of a quarter of a million people. Dozens of slaughterhouses, packing plants, laundries, and mineral reduction works plus a multitude of barns and feed lots were polluting the river. Starting in 1971, steps were taken to improve water quality by persuading industries and communities alike to install sewage-treatment plants.

The parkway concept, a planner's dream for decades, began to achieve reality in 1973 when the state legislature appropriated

105

funds to build a sloping greenbelt (called a berm) along the riverbanks to control flooding and to allow for plantings of grass, trees, and shrubs. Theoretically capable of withstanding a once-in-a-century flood, the berm has done its job so far despite the record-breaking spring runoffs of the 1980s.

While the river water still is not considered safe for swimming, it has come a long way. From widespread apathy has emerged a growing public concern, enough so that in 1980 a Jordan River Parkway Foundation was created to assume long-term responsibility for the river improvement tasks independent of government tax support. In 1986 the state legislature expanded the parkway concept by enacting the Parks and Recreation Riverway Enhancement Program with an initial appropriation of $600,000.

A wide variety of scenic and recreational developments totaling 434 acres along the river is now under the overall supervision of the State Division of Parks and Recreation. City-owned, fifteen-acre Glendale Park, between 2100 South and 1700 South, boasts the popular Glendale Golf Course and tennis courts plus a water slide and water pool complex called Raging Waters operated by a concessionaire. Just north of Glendale Park is the beginning of a jogging trail bordering the riverbank between 1700 South and California Avenue.

About a mile to the north, between California and Indiana avenues, lies long-established Jordan Park with its picnic tables, tennis courts, and the beautiful grounds of the International Peace Gardens, an arboretum planted with representative flora from a score of nations. Shaded picnic tables also are available to the public at Eighth South Park, just off Indiana Avenue.

Another mile to the north, the river enters the State Fairgounds at North Temple and 1000 West streets. A three-mile equestrian trail along the river starts here, as does a paved bicycle and jogging trail. At 1386 North Redwood Road lies the city's Rose Park Golf Course, near another course devoted to frisbee golf. Another mile brings the walker to a model plane airport, the latter financed by hobbyists who raised $10,000 for the development.

The stretch of river from 1700 South to 1000 North—about five miles—is a popular canoeing course from June through October. Also navigable are the stretch from 1000 North to the Great Salt Lake and a segment from 6400 South to 4500 South in the city of Murray. At the south end of Salt Lake County, after the river leaves Utah Lake and passes through the Jordan River Narrows, there is a two- to three-mile stretch of whitewater where kayakers sport when water levels are right. Experts only, please. Other parts of the river, by the way, can be very dangerous because of low bridges and irrigation dams.

The Provo-Jordan River Parkway Foundation has ambitious plans for the future, and municipalities along the river are cooperating. Salt Lake County has dedicated a new park on the river at 3300 South. Murray City has completed a major improvement along about a mile of riverfront, including a golf course. State-owned lands in other parts of the state are being traded for riverside land in West and South Jordan. A corridor is being negotiated in Midvale. Utah County has completed eight miles of trail from the Salt Lake County line past newly established Black Willow Park in Lehi to Utah Lake. Other trails have been completed from Utah Lake eastward up Provo Canyon, following the old railroad right of way. The federal Bureau of Reclamation plans to transfer lands along the Provo River up to Deer Creek and Jordanelle reservoirs for improved access to recreation and fishing sites. Kayakers, canoeists, and "tubers" (who bounce down the river in inflated innertubes) are already taking advantage of these improvements.

Rock formations at Kodachrome Basin State Park.

108

Kodachrome Basin State Park

Open all year
Camping, 24 units
Group camping
Picnicing

Modern restrooms, wheelchair
  accessible
Vault toilets
Off-highway vehicles, nearby
Concessionaire

Limestone spires resembling huge chimneys; camping; hiking; photography; off-highway vehicle riding.

Endowing a state park with a commercial name like "Kodachrome Basin" might seem suspiciously like free advertising, but even a brief look at that improbable place provides a simple explanation: there are not enough applicable adjectives in the dictionary to do full justice to the scene. The name Kodachrome at least offers a hint of the kaleidoscopic colors in store for visitors, although it says nothing about the fantastic forms that Nature has fabricated.

An earlier name for the basin—Chimney Rock State Reserve— refers to one of its outstanding features, the many tall and slender rock spires, but that name ignored the fabulous colors. Originally the basin was known locally as Thorley's Pasture for a rancher named Tom Thorley who ran cattle there for a while, but when the National Geographic Society sent a party into the region in 1948, its leaders were inspired to dub the little valley Kodachrome Flat after the color film which the society's magazine had by then made famous (later it became Kodachrome Basin). Color film had appeared on the market in 1935 but was not widely used by amateurs until after World War II. The *National Geographic Magazine* was one of the first publications to use Kodachrome extensively, starting in 1939.

Despite its out-of-the way location near Bryce Canyon National Park, the valley started to attract visitors as soon as it was established as a state reserve in 1963, the year it was acquired from the federal Bureau of Land Management. Seven miles off State Route 12, down a rough dirt road southeast of the village of Cannonville, the park covers 2,240 acres of extraordinary, rainbow-hued rock formations in a high, semidesert setting of great beauty. Cannonville, by the way, is named for a Mormon leader, George Q. Cannon. Local jokesters tell visitors that the first settlers wanted to call the place Shotgun because it was not big enough to be a cannon, but they were overruled by the Post Office Department. The completion of pavement on State Route 12 from Boulder to Capitol Reef National Monument in 1985 really opened the door to the region, and the numbers of visitors to the Basin since then have greatly increased (*see* Anasazi State Park for details on this route).

The park is open all year, although its elevation of 5,800 feet above sea level can make for some chilly winter days. The park's attractive campground is sheltered by towering sandstone cliffs and shaded by large junipers and piñon pines. Firewood is provided year-round for a fee, and a large group-use area with barbecue grills and electricity may be reserved in advance.

A self-guiding nature trail with numbered markers describes some of the natural history of the region. A two-mile road and a quarter-mile trail lead to a natural arch that remained unknown to the public until 1979, when the resident ranger, Tom Shakespeare, found it in a remote side canyon. The arch later was named for the ranger.

A larger and better-known double arch, named Grosvenor Arch, for a president of the National Geographic Society, is situated ten miles southeast of the park on a rough dirt road that intersects U.S. Highway 89 west of Lake Powell. Local inquiry of road conditions should be made before setting out.

Perhaps the most astonishing feature of Kodachrome Basin is the incredibly tall and slender columns of layered stone called chimney rocks, some of which look as if a strong wind would topple them. One theory advanced by geologists about their origin is that they were ancient geyser plugs, vents, or tubes that filled with limestone more resistant to erosion than the sandstone that encased them. Over the eons since they were formed, the sandstone eroded away, leaving the limestone columns standing alone.

Doubtless the original inhabitants of the region had a better explanation, as did the cowboys who used the valleys as a holding ground for cattle. They reportedly told gullible strangers who asked about the pillars that they were really petrified postholes. Certainly they are the stuff that legends are made of.

In addition to the dominant juniper and piñon, the park sup-

Kodachrome Basin State Park.

ports sagebrush, rabbitbrush, cliff rose, yucca, and prickly pear cactus, as well as native grasses and many wildflowers in season. Wildlife is limited in numbers by the absence of open water but still appears in rather surprising variety, mostly at night. Mule deer may be seen from time to time, and tracks of mountain lions are occasionally found in the more remote canyons. The most common daytime animal is the antelope ground squirrel, easily identified by its white tail, which it usually carries flat along its back. There are some gopher snakes and a few rattlers and many kinds of lizards.

Most of the birds seen there are migratory except for the resident (and noisy) piñon jays. Ravens, vultures, and golden eagles may be seen soaring high overhead most of the year.

The "accidental" dunes at Lark Dunes State Park, formed by wind blowing over mountains of mine debris.

112

Lark Dunes State Park

Vault toilets   ATV park

The 1,300 acres of peculiar sandy hills known as Lark Dunes are listed as a state park, but it is a state park in name only. The dunes could in fact have become an unusual desert garden, but instead they have been taken over by the dune-buggy and ATV (all-terrain vehicle) set as a rustic racetrack.

Situated at the edge of the eastern foothills of the Oquirrh Range, southwest of West Jordan off State Route 48 in the Salt Lake Valley, the dunes are peculiar in that they are man-made, if only accidentally. Prevailing winds out of the southwest blowing across mountains of tailings (rock debris) from the adjacent Bingham Canyon copper mine have built the dunes, grain by grain. As is the case with all wind-created dunes, the heavier particles fall first, closest to the source, while the lighter grains are carried farther downwind. The lightest of all are carried away as dust (*see* Coral Pink Sand Dunes State Park for more on this phenomenon).

Seeds blown in or carried in by birds and animals have sprouted in the dunes and have already produced a crop of rabbitbrush and other pioneer types of ground cover. Provided the terrain is not all torn up by wheels, in time other forms of vegetation no doubt will appear.

The only facilities at the park, which is administered as an adjunct of Great Salt Lake State Park, are a pair of portable latrines and some barbed-wire fences, which designate parking spaces for autos and an area for children to play in.

The great Bingham Canyon mine nearby is one of the world's largest open pit excavations. Low-grade copper ore has been hauled from it by wagons, trucks, and trains for well over a century. Its vast terraced pit is nearly two-and-a-half-miles wide at the top and half a mile deep. Closed for several years in the mid-1980s because of the low price of copper on the world market, it was reopened in 1987 after major investments in state-of-the-art processing and refining techniques. Visitors are welcome at the mine during the summer season to visit the view area and interpretive displays.

113

The Lowly Lichen — Pioneer of the Plant World

Few people other than botanists pay much attention to the more than 10,000 known species of lichens. In fact, very few can identify a lichen, even if it's growing on the doorstep. These adventurous yet inconspicuous, adaptable but fragile, humble but most remarkable pioneers of the plant world grow everywhere from the Arctic to the equator, from ocean atolls to the tops of mountains above tree line.

So widely do they vary in appearance that many lichen varieties are not readily identifiable as such. Some may be mistaken for dried moss dangling from trees, some look like succulents, and many are so tiny that their colonies may be thought to be mere chemical stains on rocks. In Iceland and Greenland, on the other hand, lichens are the dominant form of vegetation, as familiar to the inhabitants as corn is to the Kansas farmer. In much less exuberant forms, lichens even thrive in deserts.

One common northern species is called reindeer moss because it is a principal diet item for reindeer and caribou, which browse it like so much clover. It is highly nutritious, for all its dead-leaf appearance. In upper New England and elsewhere along the northern tier of states, and at high altitudes farther south, lichens often festoon trees with thick gray-green garlands called Old Man's Beard. It looks somewhat like the Spanish moss common in the Deep South but is not related (Spanish moss is not moss at all, but a member of the pineapple family).

Smaller varieties of lichens — some individuals are only pinpoint in size but occur in great masses — cover rocks, tree trunks and branches, old fences, bridges, houses, and other stone and wooden structures the world over. But they are not found in cities where there are dense concentrations of automobiles. Lichens are extremely sensitive to air pollution. Without clean air they die, a somber warning to urban dwellers that is largely ignored in this country. In England, however, lichens are watched closely for signs of atmospheric poisoning, like the caged canaries in old-time coal mines.

But what *are* lichens? In simple terms, lichens are the result of

114

an intricate blending of two quite different kinds of primitive plants which at a glance appear to have nothing to do with each other. Lichens are a living combination of an alga and a fungus, growing together in such close companionship they cannot be separated—and could not live apart if they were. They are so tightly intertwined they are able to exchange nourishment directly through their cells.

The word symbiosis was coined (in 1877) to describe the peculiar relationship of the algae and fungi that form lichens. Symbiosis means simply living together as distinguished from parasitism, in which one organism feeds upon another or deprives the other of nourishment. A further distinction is made by referring to the bond as "obligate symbiosis," meaning that this is not just a marriage of convenience but one of absolute, vital necessity to both partners in which both benefit equally.

In the alga-fungus symbiosis, there is a clear division of labor as well as mutual benefit. The fungus, being tough and resilient, can store water and resist drought. It exudes an acid that dissolves the rock or other surface it inhabits, allowing its tiny, hairlike tentacles to find firm footing. Unlike moss, most lichens are difficult to detach from rocks without damage to the organisms. People who want to decorate their gardens with lichens usually have to bring along the rocks on which they are growing.

A simple unicellular plant, the otherwise highly vulnerable algal member of the team could never survive in such a hostile environment as a bare rock surface, away from water and exposed to wind and weather. But algae are chlorophyll-producing plants and do what fungi cannot—manufacture food from air, water, and sunlight. The algae make enough for themselves and their partners, too.

The fungus member reproduces by spores like mushrooms and toadstools. The alga reproduces by simple cell division. The two processes may occur simultaneously. Some lichens at times appear to be covered with minute flower stalks, which are actually the reproductive organs of the fungus. Lichens, however, have no flowers, stems, leaves, roots, or seeds. They belong to the primitive plant form called thallophytes, the lowest of the great groups in the vegetable kingdom.

All lichens are worth close examination—under a magnifying glass or microscope if possible—for their structures are as intricate and varied as snowflakes, marvels of engineering and adaptation. One species known since Biblical times is the *manna* lichen that fed the Israelites on their wanderings in the wilderness. It is a kind of mossy lichen that grows in the deserts of the Near East, where it is often torn loose by the wind and blown into balls like tumbleweed. It is edible and is still used by nomadic people to make a kind of bread. Other lichen varieties may be edible also, but are not necessarily palatable. One common exception is called rock tripe, which can be boiled into a soup. Eskimos use it to treat the sick.

Many lichens look gray-green in color because the gray thallus (body) of the fungus partially hides the green alga. Some of the acids produced by the fungus may also color the thallus bright yellow, red, orange, white, or even black. On some islands off the coast of Maine, yellow wall lichens coat the rocks like yellow paint. Some other light-colored lichens may be mistaken for spilled plaster.

Since some lichens can be boiled to make blue and purple dyes, they were the principal source of such colors for the textile trade before the invention of aniline dyes. Litmus paper, a familiar item in chemistry laboratories the world over, is made from lichens. At the other end of the array of lichen uses, hummingbirds use lichens in building their nests, gaining camouflage effects in the process.

While it would take a small encyclopedia to list all the kinds of lichens, they may be grouped loosely into a few general categories according to their appearance. The crust (crustose) lichens, which cling closely to rock surfaces and look like a sort of scale or rust, come in many colors and are the most widespread. The foliose or coral lichens, which include reindeer moss, look like dried sponges or coral clusters, often white or ivory-colored. When wet, they become as resilient as sponges. Old Man's Beard also belongs to this category.

Before the days of modern science, lichens were thought to have magical or medicinal properties when applied directly to the part of the human body they resembled. Alternately, lichens were chosen for treatment if they somehow resembled the ailment itself. Thus in the case of hydrophobia, dog lichen was given to the victim. For jaundice, what else but an infusion of yellow wall lichen? For baldness, naturally, Old Man's Beard was supposed to stimulate hirsute activity.

Lichens are the true pioneers of the plant world, the only life-form able to make a living on naked rock. After a lichen colony has become established, it begins — very slowly — to make soil by decomposition of the rock, by accumulating dust from the wind, by its own carbohydrate production. The soil in turn makes a footing for mosses, then grasses and ferns, and finally flowering plants and trees, but the process can take centuries. It is a long and rocky road from a thallophyte to a sequoia.

Lost Creek State Park

Open all year   Boating/fishing
Camping, 15 units   Swimming
Vault toilets
245 surface acre lake; boating; water sports; primitive camping; year-round fishing.

Lost Creek Reservoir is a pretty little lake that is said to offer good trout fishing, but getting there can be a problem. After negotiating the last six miles of the very rough road into Lost Creek State Park, some visitors have been heard to say they wished it had stayed lost. That is because of the shaking the road has given their vehicles, especially motor homes and large trailers. The road is usually roughest in spring and is more readily passable later in the season, but drivers of large vehicles should inquire before setting out. In wet weather it can become virtually impassable for anything but a jeep, an ATV, a four-wheel-drive truck, or a horse.

At an elevation of 6,000 feet above sea level, Lost Creek Reservoir is at the far end of a tributary of the Weber River, thirty miles northeast of Morgan off Interstate 84. The road into the lake passes first a cement plant, then near Croyden a pair of unusual parallel, vertical limestone reefs forming a kind of chute called the Devil's Slide, a popular subject for postcards around the turn of the century.

The park has only minimal facilities and no resident ranger. It does have a paved launching ramp, an adjacent boat-trailer and auto parking area, and pit toilets, but no drinking water.

Originally Lost Creek was called Plumber's Creek for an early trapper. Later the name was changed, but sources differ on the reason for the name. One version says two trappers, Moses Tracy and Sidney Kelly, got lost there in 1855. Another story is that the creek disappears and reappears along its course, and still another says the creek dries up in summer and reappears after rainstorms.

The 345-acre lake backs up behind a 220-foot-high earth-fill dam constructed in the mid 1960s by the federal Bureau of Reclamation as a part of the huge Weber Basin Project.

Millsite State Park

Open all year   Vault toilets
Camping, 20 units   Boating/fishing
Picnicing   Golfing
Group pavilion   Swimming
Drinking water   Water activities
435 surface-acre lake; water sports; primitive camping.

Many agencies — federal, state, and local — are involved in the Ferron Watershed Project in central Utah which has resulted, among other benefits, in the development of Millsite State Park.

The park is situated on a 500-acre multipurpose reservoir four miles west of Ferron, a farming town on State Route 10 between Price and Fremont Junction. The county road to the park, paved except for the last mile, continues as a gravel road over the 10,000-foot-high Wasatch Plateau to join U.S. Highway 89 near Gunnison. It is closed in winter except for snowmobilers and cross-country skiers.

The park is most heavily used in summer, often at full capacity on weekends and holidays, but it also attracts winter anglers who fish through the ice for rainbow and cutthroat trout. With a depth of 120 feet at the dam, the water remains cold enough all summer to maintain the trout population.

The state park has piped water and picnic/camping units equipped with tables, benches, and barbecue stands in a tree-sheltered campground beside the lake. Two group shelters provide sixteen tables with benches and cooking facilities. A large overflow parking lot also is used by boat trailers.

Millsite Dam and Reservoir were built between 1969 and 1971 to provide irrigation water for farms in Castle Valley and domestic water for the city of Ferron, as well as for flood control and recreation. Participating in the project in addition to the city of Ferron are the Ferron Canal and Reservoir Company, the State Division of Wildlife Resources, the State Division of Water Resources, the U.S. Soil Conservation Service, and the State Division of Parks and Recreation.

Campground, picnic area, and boat-launching ramp at Millsite State Park.

Recently the city of Ferron and Emery County have joined forces to build a nine-hole golf course immediately adjacent to the state park. The fairways were planted and the course opened in the spring of 1989. A portable building was hauled in from Ferron to serve as a clubhouse.

Millsite takes its name from the fact that the reservoir covers the site of a much earlier development, a dam built at the turn of the century to furnish water power for a flour mill. The mill machinery later was moved to Ferron to grind grain for livestock feed. Part of the old millworks still is used to control the streamflow below the dam.

Part of the water flowing out of the reservoir is now being diverted into a canal to serve the new billion-dollar Utah Power and Light Company power plant in Castle Valley between Ferron and Castle Dale. Known as the Hunter Plant, it burns coal trucked in from the company's Cottonwood Mine thirteen miles to the northwest. When it is running at full capacity, the plant's big turbines are capable of generating 1,180,000 kilowatts of power.

After being used for steam and for cooling, some of the Millsite water then serves to irrigate crops on an experimental farm operated by faculty and students from Brigham Young and Utah State universities, who are checking the effects of the effluent water on air and on plants.

Minersville State Park

Open April-November
Camping, 29 units
Group camping
Picnicing
Drinking water
Modern restrooms

Showers
Sewage disposal
Electrical hookups
Boating/fishing
Off-highway vehicles, nearby
Swimming

1,130 surface-acre reservoir; boating; camping; year-round fishing.

Lacking any knowledge of the local weather or means of forecasting its devastating potential, the pioneer Mormon settlers around the city-to-be of Beaver in southwestern Utah did not know what the gods had in store for them when they built an irrigation dam on the Beaver River in 1860.

Spring snow melt and summer thunderstorms produced flash floods that roared down the precipitous slopes of the nearby Tushar Mountains, which rise east of the city to elevations of more than 12,000 feet above sea level. The first such flood made short work of a crude dam fashioned from dirt, rocks, and brush. A later dam built of rough lumber washed out along with the farms below it, as did another structure built of logs enclosing boulders in diamond-shaped pens or cribs.

Not only irrigation dams failed. In 1871, a dam was built west of Beaver to furnish water power for a gristmill. Water was piped from the dam through a canal and a series of hollowed-out logs to turn a waterwheel at the mill. The waterwheel turned a huge hand-chiseled millstone grinding locally grown wheat to flour and crushing rock salt hauled by wagon from a dry salt lake near Parowan, thirty miles or so to the south. The milling operation lasted a few years, then ended as abruptly as its predecessors when a flash flood took out the dam and carried away the hollow logs.

It was not until 1912-14 that a land company seeking to attract customers built a more substantial dam of compacted earth over a concrete core, and it survived to become known as the Rocky Ford Dam. Still in use, the dam took its name from an old boulder-strewn wagon crossing on the river just below the damsite.

Now known as the Minersville Reservoir from the nearby farming town of Minersville, its surface area of 1,130 acres has been administered since 1963 by the Utah Division of State Parks and Recreation, which has installed modern facilities. The 207-acre park includes twenty-nine campsites with shelters, restrooms with flush toilets, showers, drinking water, electrical outlets in the shelters, and barbecue grills. There is a paved boat-launching ramp and spaces for boat-trailer parking. The park is open year-round, but camping facilities are available only from April to November.

The lake and its tributary streams are open all year for fishing. The state operates a fish hatchery on Spring Creek, a tributary of the Beaver River just west of the city of Beaver. In addition to stocking lakes and streams over much of southern Utah, the hatchery from time to time releases some huge spawners that make their way down to the reservoir. Fish weighing up to nine pounds have been taken there, usually in early spring. Some fish go over the spillway to a pool below the dam making it a popular fishing hole at times.

The presence of large numbers of rough fish such as carp and chub resulted in the reservoir's being treated with chemicals in 1959 and 1961, followed by extensive restocking with rainbow trout. Occasionally fish die off during extreme low water years, although some survive deep in the conservation pool maintained by the Division of Wildlife Resources. The reservoir is stocked each fall with fingerling trout.

In addition to fishing, the reservoir is popular all summer for swimming, boating, and water sports. The campground also serves as a base for trips into the nearby Fishlake National Forest in the Tushar Mountains for mountain stream fishing, scenic tours, hiking, and fall hunting. Annual visitor totals at the park run upwards of 22,000.

Bypassed in recent years by Interstate 15, the city of Beaver, at an elevation of 5,895 feet above sea level, is becoming a retirement community as well as a commercial and tourist center. Elk Meadows ski resort to the east and Brian Head Resort, fifty miles to the south, offer downhill and cross-country skiing. These areas are increasingly popular with Californians looking for uncrowded conditions. The town is notable for its numerous historic buildings, particularly the former Beaver County Courthouse with its tower and bell. Built in the late 1870s, it now houses a museum, art gallery, and auditorium that serves as a theater for amateur productions.

As might be surmised, the river and city took their name from the fact that many beaver pelts were taken from the upper reaches of the river by early-day trappers. One of them, the famous frontiersman Jedediah Smith, referred to it as "Lost River," perhaps because it has no outlet to the sea but loses itself in the saline area to the northwest beyond the Black Rock Desert. In wet years, it runs intermittently into Sevier Lake—which itself disappears and reappears as precipitation totals dip and soar. Still earlier, the Spanish explorers Dominguez and Escalante camped on the Beaver River near present-day Minersville in 1776 (*see* Starvation State Park for details).

From 1872 until 1882 Beaver had a military post where some 250 soldiers contributed much to the economy while maintaining a relative peace among the diverse populations of the region. Trouble with the resident Paiute Indians started in 1871-72 when a mineral strike in the San Francisco Mountains west of the city brought on a stampede of get-rich-quick prospectors.

Friction with the Indians and between Mormons and non-Mormons became heated to the point that federal intervention was deemed necessary, so four companies of soldiers arrived to camp on the upper Beaver River. In 1873 permanent rock buildings were erected two miles east of the city and were dedicated the following year as Fort Cameron in honor of Colonel James Cameron, a hero of the Civil War. Abandoned in 1882, the fort was sold to the Mormon church and others for a fraction of its original cost. For decades it served as a private school. The grounds are now occupied by a racetrack, municipal playgrounds, and some private real-estate developments.

Besides the city of Beaver, several other farming communities sprang up in the vicinity of the reservoir in the latter half of the nineteenth century. Minersville, on State Route 130 southwest of the state park, has some early dwellings of interest to history buffs and is a producer of beef and dairy cattle, fruit, corn, and early garden vegetables.

Adamsville, at the north end of the reservoir, was first settled in 1867 by one David B. Adams. Iron was produced at the site, giving it its original name of Beaver Iron Works. It was also known as Wales for the many Welsh families that settled there.

Wind ruffles lake surface at Minersville State Park.

West of Minersville, State Route 21 passes through the railroad towns of Milford and the ghost town of Frisco before threading the Wah Wah Mountains to join U.S. Highways 6 and 50 just over the Nevada state line.

View south from Utah border on Monument Valley highway.

126

Monument Valley State Park

Monument Valley State Park would be hard to find right now (early 1988) because it has never really existed as a park except on paper. To date it has no facilities whatever. No signs point to it, no fences fix its boundaries, and there is nothing at all to separate it from the fantastic scenery that surrounds it on the Navajo Reservation.

However, at least on paper, Monument Valley State Park consists of some twenty acres of land down on the Utah-Arizona border, where U.S. Highway 163 crosses the state line in Monument Valley, about halfway between Kayenta, Arizona, and Mexican Hat, Utah. The park's center, if it had one, would be right at the intersection of a paved country road that runs roughly east and west. Funds permitting in the future, the State Division of Parks plans to set up a public information booth at the intersection, perhaps to be staffed by local English-speaking Navajos.

Eastward the road runs four miles to the well-developed Navajo Tribal Park with its assortment of tourist attractions. To the west, the same road provides access to Goulding's Trading Post and Lodge, another major tourist attraction, and continues another ten miles to the hamlet of Oljeto. Oljeto is a combination trading post and school established long ago by the pioneering Wetherill family, some of whose members were enthusiastic amateur archaeologists, one of whom discovered the great cliff dwellings at Mesa Verde in Colorado.

Long ago all of Monument Valley north of the state line, including some of its most spectacular vertical scenery, was part of a poorly defined region known as the Paiute Strip, which in turn was part of a larger Paiute Indian reservation. Through one of the vagaries of government action, the Strip was returned to the public domain by an act of Congress in 1892.

Then in 1908 an executive order signed by President Theodore Roosevelt reestablished the Strip as a reservation for various Indian groups, but in the interim some ranchers had moved in and a protracted legal battle ensued. The executive order was revoked in 1922 and the land returned to the public domain (thus open to homesteading) once more, only to be withdrawn again in 1929 and handed back to the Indians.

Finally, on March 3, 1933, an act of Congress added the Paiute Strip to the already huge Navajo Indian reservation and so it remains today, minus a few parcels such as the state park land, Goulding's resort, the adjacent hospital, and the private holdings at Oljeto. Meanwhile the remaining Paiute either had moved away to more fertile lands elsewhere or had been assimilated by marriage into the Navajo tribe.

It was during one of those on-again, off-again periods of public domain in Monument Valley that a young Colorado sheepman named Harry Goulding was able to buy a 640-acre section from the government for 50 cents an acre. That was in 1923, after Goulding had wandered over much of Monument Valley on horseback, on foot, and in one of the first automobiles to venture into that remote and little-known region.

Born in Durango, Colorado, in 1897, Goulding was raised on a ranch near Aztec, New Mexico. After serving in the army in World War I as a muleteer (mule skinner), Goulding wandered into Monument Valley in 1919 looking for some lost sheep. He resolved to make his home there and finally returned in 1923 with his new bride and built a rock house which was to develop into a trading post and lodge in the narrow canyon under Rock Door Mesa. There he remained for forty years, becoming one of the few Anglo-Americans ever to be accepted as a friend by the old-time Navajos.

For a few years Goulding ran sheep in the valley, then became a full-time licensed Indian trader. He traded food, clothing, and other merchandise for Navajo rugs and silver, much of which he accepted as pawn. Some of the more valuable work he loaned money on over and over again, never selling it.

In addition to serving as a mentor and advisor to the Navajo in their dealings with local, state, and federal bureaucrats, Goulding donated a piece of land across from the trading post as a site for a missionary clinic. He was also instrumental in persuading the government to add the region north of the state line to the Navajo reservation in 1933. But perhaps his most notable and certainly his most widely publicized achievement was his successful effort to bring movie companies to Monument Valley during the Great Depression of the 1930s.

Seeking a source of ready cash for his literally starving Navajo friends, in 1938 he persuaded an acquaintance to prepare a large selection of photographs of the valley. Armed with the photos, he went to Hollywood and camped on the doorstep of the MGM studio until he finally gained the reluctant attention of someone in authority.

At first nobody would believe that such scenery existed in the United States, but once he was able to convince the movie moguls that the photos were not faked, Goulding's mission bore fruit in abundance. Starting with the classic film *Stagecoach* in late 1938, director John Ford employed hundreds of Navajos in a long series of Western horse operas, including such well-known feature-length productions as *Fort Apache, The Searchers*, and *Cheyenne Autumn*. Many other films, from *Billy the Kid* (starring Robert Taylor, 1941) to *The Eiger Sanction* (Clint Eastwood, 1975) have also been shot in the valley by other directors.

Interrupted by World War II, film making continued well into the 1950s, the widespread use of color adding new zest to the scenery. Anyone who missed these spectaculars when they first appeared on the screen no doubt has seen some of them since on the late-late-night TV shows.

Perhaps because of its strategic location and the fact that it was privately owned, the future site of the state park was used as a base camp for many of the movies made in the valley. The entire town of Tombstone (Arizona) was erected in 1946 on the site for Ford's filming of *My Darling Clementine*, much to the confusion of at least one casual tourist who strayed into the valley by chance.

Goulding put up tents for some of the early moviemakers and later added some stone cabins, which became the nucleus of the present-day resort. When *She Wore a Yellow Ribbon* was filmed by Ford in 1949, permanent buildings later used for a medical clinic were constructed. The clinic was eventually established in 1950 across from Goulding's lodge on land he donated to the Seventh-Day Adventist Church, and it has since expanded into a full-scale medical facility. Until it opened, the nearest hospital had been at Tuba City 106 miles away over a poor road. An airstrip built by Goulding for his guests also provides emergency air service for the hospital; it has served in numerous life-threatening situations.

The many Monument Valley movies plus improved roads have brought an ever-increasing flow of tourist traffic to the area. To

Navajo horses running free in Monument Valley.

meet the growing demand for accommodations, Goulding built more cabins, later adding a restaurant and service station to his trading post, which had meanwhile grown into a general store. Today, Goulding's is a first-class modern tourist facility, although it is Goulding's in name only. Goulding and his wife, Leone, donated the property to Knox College of Galesburg, Illinois, in 1963, in return for a life income. The purpose of the gift was to provide scholarships for Navajo college students.

Goulding died in Cottonwood, Arizona, in 1981, at the age of eighty-four. His widow, at the time this account was written, was residing at Page, Arizona. Knox College has since sold the property to the LaFonte brothers, former owners of Thunderbird Lodge at Canyon de Chelly.

The four-wheel-drive expeditions into the unmapped back country of Monument Valley that Goulding began back in the 1940s still continue, a major attraction for tourists. In recent years a fully equipped RV park and campground with hot showers and a store have been added to the lodge, as well as a row of new air-conditioned motel units. Meals are served cafeteria style at the lodge, which is open from mid-March to mid-November. The trading post still carries Navajo rugs and jewelry.

Lone spire framed by juniper tree in Monument Valley.

132

Moonlight Magic in Monument Valley

It is easy these days to zip through Monument Valley on the main highway in fifteen or twenty minutes, but doing so seems close to blasphemy, like running a drag race through the Elysian Fields. The briefest of encounters with that wild and lovely expanse of brilliant red and yellow sandstone sculpture can be a mindboggling experience, especially at dawn or at sundown.

By the light of a full moon, that ancient eroded valley is like nothing else on earth. I saw it once at such a time of magic more than a quarter of a century ago, and the recollection still haunts me. Let me try to describe the scene:

Sitting around a campfire early one chilly March evening, we three men were making idle wagers about the exact spot on the distant skyline where the full moon would appear—the whole reason we were there. We had slogged for miles through hub-deep mud in four-wheel drive to get to that special spot at that particular time, and we were wondering if it had been worth the effort.

In the eerie golden half-light of the evening afterglow, the panorama before us was like a moonscape, a vast plain studded with skyscraping spires and turrets and towers topped with purple and orange flame by the dying rays of the sun at our backs. Just at dusk a flock of sheep and goats, their bells tinkling, wandered by, followed by a big shaggy dog and a tiny Navajo girl in a long satin skirt. The girl and the dog paused briefly at the edge of the firelight to stare at us in evident wonder, and then they vanished as silently as they had appeared.

Suddenly, with no more warning than a brief flash under a low cloud bank on the eastern horizon, the moon burst into view, a great shining orb on the rim of the world.

It rose huge and fast, an illusion magnified by the vast distance, the crystalline air, the pancake flatness of the terrain between the stone pillars. It came up so quickly we almost forgot to snap the shutters of the cameras we had set up on tripods for the purpose. Even the soft click of the camera shutters seemed a sacrilege, and none of us could utter a word.

The moon rose in the most improbable of places, precisely

133

Ephemeral rainwater pond after Monument Valley storm.

between two of the spires of those soaring red sandstone towers aptly called "The Mittens," one of the myriad fantastic formations that give the valley its name.

It is said that at sunset on a clear summer day, the shadows of the Mittens stretch out more than thirty miles across the desert. It is said that on hot days the rabbits and the coyotes and the lizards line up single file in a state of truce in the narrow shadows of the Mittens, waiting in the shade for the sun to go down.

I do not know about these things from my own experience, but I find these ideas no more incredible than the valley itself. I do know that the broad, ink-black moon shadows cast by the Mittens, and the butter-yellow wedge of moonlight shining between them, at once enveloped our camp. There was no sound.

At one stage early in its ascent, the moon seemed to pause for an instant, as if pinioned on a spire jutting from the side of the nearest Mitten. Then it broke loose and rose again in a curving course that soon carried it above and away from the pinnacles entirely. A quick breeze brought up a thin cloud veil that obscured the sky, as if to announce that we had seen enough for one night, as indeed we had. It was almost a relief to have the curtain drawn on the celestial scene.

If you would have such an experience for yourself, be in Monument Valley some night when a full moon is due. It is an easy place to get to now, the main roads all paved, good accommodations nearby. The Navajo tribal campground is there, facing east as all Navajo dwelling places do. The little Navajo girl and her sheep and her goats and her big shaggy dog might be there, too, for I suspect they have always been there, at least in spirit.

Then wait for the moon to rise between the Mittens, and if you see it as I saw it so long ago, you will not forget it all the rest of your days. You may even be privileged to hear the music, as I still can, the muted trumpets, the muffled clash of cymbals, the voices of the heavenly choir.

The Mittens frame moonrise in Monument Valley.

Visitor views informative panel at Newspaper Rock State Park.

138

Newspaper Rock State Park

Open all year
Camping, 8 units
Picnicing
Indian petroglyphs; photography.

Vault toilets
Off-highway vehicles, nearby

Newspaper Rock State Park straddles the main highway into the Needles District of Canyonlands National Park, but the chances are that most motorists whiz right through the little park with only a glance at its main attraction. State Route 211 bisects the park twelve miles west of U.S. Highway 191, which connects Moab and Monticello.

Those hurrying travelers miss one of the finest displays of Indian rock art to be found anywhere in the United States, and one of the few such arrays that can be seen at close range, only a few steps from a parking lot. There are many other panels to be seen in the park as well. It seems almost a miracle that the art has survived, so close to a highway, with only minor evidence of vandalism.

The detailed main picture panel also provides a rare opportunity for close-up photography. Facing southwest, part of the panel is in full sun in late afternoon. All of the myriad figures are *petroglyphs* (pecked in the rock face) rather than *pictographs* (painted on). A plaque interprets some of the figures.

Across the highway from the rock art display is a small campground beside Indian Creek, a perennial stream originating in the Abajo Mountains to the south and flowing northwest to the Colorado River. The water of Indian Creek is not considered potable, so campers must bring their own. The campground is densely shaded by native cottonwoods, box elders, junipers, oaks, and piñon pines. At an elevation of 6,080 feet above sea level, it is not used much in winter when the access road sometimes is snowpacked, but it is popular the rest of the year.

Not far away on Indian Creek is the Dugout Ranch, for years the headquarters of one of the great cattle empires in the world. As the Indian Creek Cattle Company, later the Scorup-Somerville

Cattle Company, the complex of ranches extended over much of southeastern Utah. Much of the land was eventually sold to members of the Redd family, who still run cattle in the area.

In addition to the rock art, a short self-guided nature trail starts at the parking lot, loops through the campground, and returns to the picture panel, giving visitors information on geological and botanical features. When the park was established in 1966, it was called Indian Creek State Historical Monument. The name was changed to Newspaper Rock State Historical Monument in 1974, and in 1983 it became Newspaper Rock State Park. Prior to the paving of the route to Canyonlands National Park, the display was little known and seldom visited. None of the early Spanish explorers or later American trappers, prospectors, or ranchers appear to have mentioned it in their accounts.

The cliffs themselves are an interesting study in geology. The thick white top layer is Navajo sandstone, next below is Kayenta sandstone, and the lowest layer is Wingate sandstone. All are believed to be remnants of massive sand dunes heaped up by wind 200 to 700 million years ago during the Triassic and Jurassic ages. Dinosaur tracks from the Jurassic period are visible, preserved in the sandstone, in a dry wash a quarter mile to the west.

The rock art is difficult for modern man to comprehend, let alone interpret, and the reasoning and intent of the prehistoric artists responsible for the pictures must remain largely guesswork. Accurate dating isn't even possible, although within broad limits some of the work can be related to historical events. For example, a few figures depict men on horseback shooting arrows at deer. Since there were no horses in the Southwest before the arrival of the Spaniards late in the sixteenth century, those petroglyphs must be relatively recent. Unlike the Anasazi ruins throughout the region, rock art has been a continuing process practiced until very recently. Some scholars believe that some southwestern tribal members are still creating rock art, and the entire question of dating and interpreting the figures is the subject of lively scientific inquiry.

There is another way, however, to learn something about the age of the drawings. All of them are pecked or scratched through the dark brown patina called desert varnish, which is a coating on smooth rock surfaces caused by oxidation of some of the minerals in the rock, a process that takes centuries, if not millennia. The

Petroglyph display at Newspaper Rock State Park. (Note six-toed feet.)

etchings or carvings expose the lighter rock beneath the surface layer. Thus the crude scratchings of modern-day vandals become obvious since their color is much lighter than the older art. Most of the fools' names have been erased by park officials.

At the top of the cluster of figures at Newspaper Rock are two that appear to be much older than the rest, since they have become much darker by the same chemical reaction that produces the varnish. They are so high up on the rock they may have been pecked when the flood plain at the foot of the rock was much higher than it is now. Even with continued protection from vandals, eventually all of the figures will become less distinct and all but disappear, but not for a very long time indeed.

Visitors with lively imaginations can interpret the drawings any way they choose; some have seen them as the products of casual doodling, of religious fervor, of a visitation by creatures from outer space. So far nobody has come up with a satisfactory explanation for the figures of men with six toes, found all over the Southwest as well as at Newspaper Rock. Perhaps there was once a race of people who actually had six toes on each foot and were therefore venerated as deities. In any case, the modern name Newspaper Rock may not be too far off the mark, for the panel does seem to depict some sort of news reporting by a people who never reached the stage of writing but had something they felt obliged to report, a kind of testimony in stone.

Robert D. Young of the Otter Creek Reservoir Company. Photo courtesy of Mrs. Revo M. Young, Richfield, Utah.

Otter Creek State Park

Open all year   Modern restrooms, wheelchair
Camping, 24 units   accessible
Group camping   Showers
Picnicing   Boating/fishing
Drinking water   Swimming
2,500 surface-acre reservoir; boating; camping; year-round fishing.

Some of Utah's best bird watching is an unusual fringe benefit of 80-acre Otter Creek State Park, which borders the south end of a reservoir on a tributary of the Sevier River four miles north of the old mining town of Antimony, west of Capitol Reef National Park.

There, in addition to excellent fishing, boating, camping, and winter ice fishing, may be seen a wide variety of resident and migratory birds, including sandhill cranes, many kinds of ducks, Canada geese, whistling swans, gulls, plovers, sandpipers, and a host of eagles, turkey vultures, and songbirds.

This remarkable concentration of avian visitors may be due, at least in part, to the lake's relative isolation on a secondary state highway (State Route 62) between high plateaus. The long, narrow lake backs up behind a forty-foot-high earth-fill, rock-faced dam built by the Mormon farmers of the region for irrigation purposes in the 1890s, a monumental undertaking for the time. Now, however, the lake's multiple recreational attractions have greatly superseded its original purpose, at least in the minds of its users. Modern facilities consist of twenty-four campsites with shade trees, shaded tables and grills, central restrooms with showers, a sewage disposal station, and a fish-cleaning sink. Also there are ample overflow camp spaces with more primitive facilities. A paved boat ramp and a floating dock adjoin the campground.

Open to fishing all year, the cold waters of the lake support some trophy-size rainbow and cutthroat trout and some big hybrids weighing upwards of twelve pounds. A large pool below the dam is popular with fly fishermen. The total number of visitors is estimated to be more than 60,000 annually, with the greatest concentration during the summer, when the park's elevation of nearly 6,400 feet above sea level attracts refugees from valley heat. The park also serves as a base camp for deer, antelope, and elk hunters during fall hunting seasons.

About thirty miles north of the dam, State Route 62 intersects State Route 24, the main access route eastward to Capitol Reef National Park. A good gravel road south of Antimony leads to Bryce Canyon National Park, forty miles away.

There are no road signs or historical markers to inform visitors that the lake they are enjoying is itself a tribute to an almost superhuman effort by its originators, who had no time ever to go fishing or hunting except for food and who were born far too early to know about water-skiing or outboard motors.

Of the many, often desperate, irrigation projects undertaken by Utah's pioneer agriculturalists before the turn of the century, few would appear to have had less chance for success or even completion than the dam and reservoir proposed by the Otter Creek Reservoir Company in the mid-1890s.

The drought-ridden farmers of the region knew a little bit about digging canals, but nothing at all about large-scale dam building, and they had little money to risk in such an uncertain venture, however much they might have needed the water. Many heated meetings had to be held before the leaders of nine separate local canal companies could agree on where and how to build a dam.

After a site was finally selected, the group applied for water rights just three days ahead of a Texas-based company that wanted to take all of the surplus water from the Sevier River and its tributaries as far downstream as the Millard County line.

When the Otter Creek Reservoir officers applied for an $18,000 loan to buy the land the projected reservoir would flood, no bank in Utah would lend a nickel. At this juncture, six of the directors walked out of a crucial meeting, declaring that the whole scheme was hopeless. Undaunted, the remaining four directors voted to proceed, on the shaky grounds that a quorum had been present when the meeting started and it had not been officially adjourned! One of the remaining four, Robert Dixon Young, a native of Scotland who grew up in Richfield, was chosen to supervise the job, although he had no previous experience in dam building and no engineering background.

Thirty years old at the time, Young volunteered to serve without pay, since there was no money to pay him or anyone else. He moved with his pregnant wife and two small children into a tumbledown cabin overlooking the damsite. Mrs. Young agreed to cook for the workers if they would furnish the food, and she even promised that she and the children would wash all the dishes.

Two state engineers arrived to inspect the site. Young put them up at the area's only hotel, nine miles away in the town of Kingston, paying for the room and meals with the last $2.50 he had. He slept in a haystack, explaining that his health would not allow him to sleep or eat inside. His wife had provided him with a hamper of food.

After inspecting the proposed damsite, the two men said the job would require machinery costing anywhere from $25,000 to $100,000. They laughed when Young told them there was no money at all and that the project was entirely dependent on local volunteer labor and homemade equipment.

When ground was broken for the Otter Creek Reservoir on October 19, 1897, the construction "crew" consisted of one man and three boys. Wages were eighteen cents an hour for workers and thirty-two cents an hour for a man and a team, payable in shares in the reservoir company or in one of the nine participating canal companies. Many of the farmers were too busy to come themselves but sent their boys instead.

Some of the workers slept in a bunkhouse and ate with the Youngs, but most of them simply camped out for weeks and even months at a time. Those who had extra provisions brought them along for the common kitchen.

Lacking any kind of heavy machinery for doing such difficult jobs as clearing a bog full of tangled roots, the men devised their own. A plough attached to the middle of a logging chain was dragged across the swamp by a team of horses and back the other way by another team. Men worked in mud "up to their armpits" keeping the plough on course.

The dissenting members of the board of directors tried a few times to stop the work, but Young told them, "These people are fighting for water and there's no water to get. We're going ahead with this reservoir."

Just when the options the group held on the ranchland that was to be inundated were about to run out, a bank in the town of

Mt. Pleasant negotiated a loan through a New York bank for $18,000 in February 1898. Soon other banks followed suit, and Young was then able to acquire a wood-fired donkey engine to help with the heavy work.

A spillway 274 feet long was driven through the solid rock cliff at one end of the dam and lined with cement. Two control gates and an overflow spillway were installed. When the company's directors finally came to inspect the nearly completed project, water was backed up for miles. Seeing water actually flowing from the outlet tunnel, the directors were so jubilant that they voted to pay Young $2.50 a day from then on—there was no mention of back pay—and they also agreed to pay a $300 lumber bill. Soon dozens of volunteer men and teams were on the job to help in the final stages of the work.

Over the solidly packed core of clay and earth held in place by timber pilings driven by a homemade pile driver, thousands of tons of rock, hauled in by wagons, were added. Some of the boulders were so large that each one was a wagonload. Smaller rocks were used for riprapping the dam's surface.

When the job was done, the state engineers who were called to inspect it said it was "one of the best and more secure earth reservoir dams in the country." They judged well, for the dam has held ever since.

In recent years the state has improved the dam and spillways at a cost of around half a million dollars. A new control tower operates hydraulic gates. A new diversion canal has been built around the head of the lake to prevent overflowing. But the basic structure, started nearly a hundred years ago by one man and three boys, remains intact.

After the completion of the Otter Creek project and another one at Piute Lake farther down the Sevier River, Young remained in the construction business. He served as vice-president of the International Irrigation Congress at St. Louis in 1919, and in 1922 he accompanied a group of government engineers on a survey trip down the Colorado River looking for damsites.

A staunch Mormon, Young remained active after retirement, working in the offices of the Church of Jesus Christ of Latter-day Saints in Salt Lake City. He died June 12, 1962, a month short of his ninety-fifth birthday.

How the Sego Lily Saved the Settlers

There must be many reasons, some obvious, some obscure, many long-forgotten, for selecting certain flowers to represent the states of the union. Probably the most common reason is the sheer abundance of the native blossoms, such as the Colorado columbine, the California poppy, and the bluebonnet of Texas, to name but a few.

None of these have a more compelling reason for selection than Utah's handsome white Sego lily, the plant that quite literally saved many Mormons from starving during the terrible winters of the late 1840s. It was not the blossom itself that played such a vital role, but the plant's sweet and succulent bulb that sustained the settlers in their time of direst need.

Following the example of the local Indians, the pioneers gathered the walnut-size bulbs by the sackful, ate them raw, boiled them like potatoes, or ground them into flour for bread. It is said that an early English botanist who wanted to collect a number of the bulbs hired some local Indian women to dig them up for him. He soon had to pay the women with bacon and flour to keep them from eating the bulbs as fast as they dug them up.

That Englishman may well have been Thomas Nuttall, a famous nineteenth-century botanist and ornithologist who gave the plant its Latin name—*Calochortus nuttallii*. (*Calochortus* means "beautiful herb," which it certainly is.) Curator of Harvard's botanical garden from 1822 to 1832, Nuttall accompanied several scientific expeditions to the Far West before returning to his native England in 1842. He is credited with identifying many new species of American plants, some of which now bear his name.

Besides humans, animals, from mice to bears, also foraged on the bulbs. Probably the only reason the plants were not exterminated by the wholesale assault staged by the Mormons, the Indians, and the wild creatures of the region is that the flower quickly withers, stem and all, after it has bloomed. All that is left above ground is an inconspicuous seed pod, which is quickly gobbled up by birds and rodents when they can find it.

Outside Utah, the Sego lily is generally called Mariposa lily or

147

Sego lily or Mariposa tulip (Calochortus Nuttallii), *one of fifty-seven varieties.*

tulip, also star tulip and butterfly tulip. The fifty-seven species of *Calochortus* grow entirely in the West, ranging from California to the Dakotas, as far north as Canada and as far south as Guatemala, from the Mojave Desert to the Rocky Mountain timberline. The nine varieties found in the Rocky Mountain states range in color from brilliant yellow to deep purple, from pure white to pale green, and are decorated with spots, bands, and stripes in contrasting hues. Most species bloom in June or July, earlier in the desert and as late as the first frost in alpine regions.

A true lily, each flower of the Mariposa has three petals, three sepals, and six stamens. Some grow nearly two feet tall; others, aptly called weak-stemmed, cannot hold their heads up but writhe along the ground. Most species, including the lilies of Utah, stand about eight or ten inches high, usually with one flower to a stem.

One species found in the southwestern deserts is there called Noona but is generally known as the green-banded Mariposa. It has a vertical green stripe running down the center of each lilac-tinted petal. The bulb of this variety is said to be particularly delicious, which no doubt is why it is hard to find.

The name Sego, a word of Shoshone or Ute Indian origin, appears on the map of Utah in a canyon and a ghost town northeast of Crescent Junction off Interstate 70. Now deserted, Sego had been a coal-mining camp from the turn of the century until the coming of diesel locomotives ended the lucrative railroad market for coal. The road to Sego passes through Sego Canyon, where some badly vandalized Indian pictographs and petroglyphs may be seen on the cliffs.

Sego achieved a degree of fame in the 1930s when mine officials shipped the casts of two huge dinosaur tracks to the American Museum of Natural History. The museum sent an expedition to the region in 1937 and found the footprints of a dinosaur with a fifteen-foot stride estimated to have stood thirty-five feet high.

Shallow water and a floating tree trunk form a children's playground at Palisade State Park.

150

Palisade State Park

Open April-November
Camping, 53 units
Group camping
Picnicing
Group pavilion
Drinking water
Modern restrooms, wheelchair accessible

Showers
Sewage disposal
Boating/fishing
Golfing
Off-highway vehicles, nearby
Swimming

Camping; nonpower boating; swimming; year-round fishing; hiking; 9-hole golf course.

Palisade Lake's modern facilities offer no hint of the seventy-acre lake's century-long, colorful history as a popular public playground. Not even a trace remains of the excursion railroad that once brought throngs to the lake, nor of the steamboats that plied its waters, nor of the dance pavilion and the cabins that were major attractions late into the Roaring Twenties.

It is easy to see why the little lake has been so popular, not only because of its beautiful wooded setting on the western slope of the Wasatch Plateau, but because of its pleasant summer climate at an elevation of 5,800 feet above sea level. The park is just south of the city of Manti on U.S. 89 in the center of the state, and it attracts more than 60,000 visitors a year, most of them during the summer months. The lake is open for fishing year-round, but the overnight campground facilities are open only from April to November. There is a boat launching ramp for nonpower boats.

It all started back in the 1860s when Daniel B. Funk, an early settler of the surrounding Sanpete Valley, dreamed up a scheme to create a summer resort and weekend playground. With the assistance and encouragement of Brigham Young, he obtained a deed to the property from Chief Arrapine of the resident Sanpitch Indians, a Ute group that gave its name, somewhat changed, to the valley. Funk and his family built a dam on Sixmile Creek and a canal to the lake site, an exceedingly difficult task in the days before power equipment, and by 1873 had succeeded in creating a reservoir about twenty feet deep.

Parade of domestic geese at Palisade Lake.

In the next several years he added a dance hall and some rental cabins, planted shade trees, and provided facilities for bathing, fishing, rowboating, picnicing, and the like. People came from miles around by horse and buggy and on horseback. In winter Funk cut ice on the lake and stored it in sawdust to use in making ice cream. A large plateful of the confection then sold for five cents.

In 1894 the Sanpete Valley Railway Company built a branch line to bring passenger train service within 500 yards of the lake shore. Earlier, a steam-powered pleasure boat that had provided excursion rides capsized in 1881, drowning eleven passengers, most of them children. After World War I a second steam launch, this one carrying only six passengers, plied the lake for several years.

After Funk's death in 1887, the resort passed through a series of owners including one group in the 1920s that changed the name to Palisade Lake, from a fancied resemblance of the cliffs that overlook the lake to the Palisades along the Hudson River, where the owners had once lived.

The onset of the Great Depression in the 1930s, plus the advent of modern automobiles and highways, led to the gradual decline of the lake's popularity. A fire destroyed the dance pavilion and it was never rebuilt. Gasoline rationing during World War II put the lake beyond the reach of most pleasure-seekers.

After World War II, the lake regained some of its visitorship for its fishing, swimming, and winter ice skating. Sanpete County donated sixty-two acres of lakeshore to the state park system in 1964, and the adjacent nine-hole golf course in 1986. The lake's depth has been increased from twenty to forty feet to provide additional water for irrigation and recreation.

Palisade State Park is situated just east of Sterling, a small farming community six miles south of historic Manti, the seat of Sanpete County. Manti is one of the oldest Mormon settlements in Utah outside Salt Lake City and is named for a city mentioned in the Book of Mormon. The Mormon Miracle Pageant is staged on the grounds of the Manti Temple every summer. East of Manti, a graded road leads up to scenic Skyline Drive, which runs north and south along the 10,000-foot summit of the Wasatch Plateau, where there are many Forest Service campgrounds.

"This Is the Place" monument at Pioneer Trail State Park.

Pioneer Trail State Park

Open all year
Day-use only
Picnicing
Museum
Drinking water

Modern restrooms, wheelchair
   accessible
Cross-country skiing
Concessionaire

Living history museum; Old Deseret pioneer community; This the Place Monument.

There may be no better way to comprehend the dramatic history of the Mormon emigration to Utah in the mid-nineteenth century than to spend some time at Pioneer Trail State Park on the northeastern edge of the Salt Lake Valley. Essentially an indoor-outdoor historic museum, Pioneer Trail comprises four areas, three of them devoted to the saga of the Mormons and their heroic struggle to create a community in the midst of a wilderness. The fourth area, called Rotary Glen, is a heavily used municipal park and picnic ground close to the visitor center.

Established in 1957, Pioneer Trail is one of the oldest state parks and one of the most popular, judging by the annual visitor total of more than half a million. It is by all odds the most complex of all the state parks, relating in statuary, murals, exhibits, and restored pioneer buildings the story of Utah's development from 1776 to 1869.

Dominating the park is the great This is the Place Monument, a granite and bronze sculpture dedicated July 24, 1947, to commemorate the arrival of the first Mormon settlers a century earlier. Just east of the monument is the mouth of Emigration Canyon, from which the first party of settlers emerged on July 22, 1847. Brigham Young arrived in a carriage two days later, ill with mountain fever. Scanning the great valley below, he supposedly said, "It is enough. This is the right place, drive on." The monument was listed in 1961 on the National Landmark Register.

Designed by Mahonri M. Young, a grandson of Brigham Young, the monument is a stone tower eighty-six feet long and sixty feet high. The tower has three clusters of bronze figures

155

sixteen feet high. The group on the monument's north side represents the trappers and fur traders who explored most of Utah's rivers and streams between 1820 and 1840. The south group shows the party of Spanish priests Dominguez and Escalante, who explored much of what is now Utah in 1776. The central group atop the monument depicts the Mormon leaders Brigham Young, Heber C. Kimball, and Wilford Woodruff viewing the Salt Lake Valley.

In the visitor center immediately to the north of the monument, a large mural in three panels illustrates the major events in the 1846-47 emigration of the Mormons from Nauvoo, Illinois, to the Salt Lake Valley. The mural was painted in 1959 by well-known artist Lynn Fausett, a native of Utah.

One mural section depicts the Mormon trek westward starting in February 1846 when they left Nauvoo because of continued persecution. The central mural shows Brigham Young being advised by the famous western scout Jim Bridger about the route they were to follow and the nature of the region where the Mormons planned to settle. The third panel shows the pioneers preparing their wagons for the difficult descent of the steep, brush-choked canyon just east of the Salt Lake Valley. Also in the visitor center are public restrooms, a shop where gifts and souvenirs are sold, and a small auditorium where a seven-minute audio presentation tells the story of the Mormon emigration.

North of the visitor center is the area known as Old Deseret. Deseret is a term from the Book of Mormon meaning honey bee, a symbol of industriousness. The original name for Utah was the State of Deseret, but Congress made the region "Utah Territory" because it thought the name was "too Mormon." Still being developed, Old Deseret is a fascinating collection of pioneer buildings, many of them transported from their original sites elsewhere in the state and chosen to represent and interpret life in Utah before the arrival of the railroad in 1869. Some have been reconstructed, others restored as nearly as possible to their original condition.

Brigham Young's Forest Farmhouse, moved to the park from its original site four miles to the southwest, was one of several homes the Mormon leader maintained in the territory. Restored in 1969 by the LDS church, it was open to the public as a museum from 1970 to 1974, then was traded to the State of Utah for Brigham Young's winter home in St. George and moved to Old

Deseret. At its original site the farmhouse served as headquarters for a 640-acre dairy farm and an experimental agricultural station where sugar beets, silkworms, and alfalfa were raised.

Other pioneer structures in Old Deseret include a reconstruction of the Social Hall, a large building dedicated in 1853 as the center of Salt Lake City's social and public activities. Half adobe and half sandstone, the two-story building served as a theater, a banquet hall, a school, and once as a meeting place for the Territorial Legislature. The original building on Social Hall Avenue downtown was torn down in 1922, but its replica is faithful to the original design. Social Hall now is available for rental by private groups.

An illustrated brochure available at the visitor center describes the additional dozen or more pioneer structures to be seen at Old Deseret. Guided tours of the village are offered every day of the week May through October and on a limited basis the rest of the year. The tours are free but donations are accepted.

During holidays and all summer, activities of pioneer life like butter-churning, quilting, gardening, weaving, and soap and candle making are demonstrated by trained interpreters in costume of the period. Special programs are presented for Halloween, Thanksgiving, and the Christmas season.

Outside the park complex, thirty-six miles of Mormon Trail from the edge of the city to Henefer have been designated by the National Park Service as a part of the National Trail System. Henefer, a hamlet at the junction of Interstate 84 and State Route 65, is the spot where the Donner-Reed party of 1846 turned southwestward from Weber Canyon (*see* East Canyon State Park for the story of their terrible travail).

Even after the coming of the railroad, the Mormon Trail was used for another decade or so by emigrants. An estimated 70,000 church members, many from the British Isles and Scandinavia, arrived on the trail between 1847 and 1869. Some 3,000 of them, too poor to afford ox-drawn wagons, hauled their possessions across the Great Plains and Rocky Mountains in handcarts in the 1850s. Freight wagons also plied the trail with supplies and trade goods, and missionaries followed it eastward to cross the Atlantic seeking converts.

Interpretive sites have been developed and more are planned along the route from Henefer. An illustrated folder prepared by

Brigham Young's Forest Farmhouse, restored and moved to Pioneer Trail State Park.

the National Park Service and available at the Pioneer Trail visitor center describes the entire 1,300-mile route of the Mormons westward from the Mississippi River.

Piute State Park

Open all year   Boating/fishing
Camping   Off-highway vehicles, nearby
Vault toilets   Swimming
Primitive camping; water activities; rock hounding.

Although it is visible and easily accessible from U.S. Highway 89 between Junction and Marysvale north of Bryce Canyon National Park, only a roadside signboard identifies Piute Lake as a state park. One of Utah's largest artificial lakes, it offers only minimal public facilities. At a cool 6,000 feet elevation, its waters are well stocked with trout and it is popular with fishermen both above and below the dam.

The dam was built in 1908 by the same man, Robert D. Young, who built Otter Creek Dam (*see* Otter Creek State Park for his amazing story), but this time he had the blessing and financial backing of the state. The reservoir is on the main fork of the Sevier River near Junction, seat of tiny Piute County. The town features a charming red-brick courthouse of 1902-1908 vintage and several other buildings dating from the same period. The county is named for the once-dominant native people, the Southern Paiute, a tribe of Shoshonean stock. (The name has also been spelled Pahute and Pah-Ute, but Paiute is the spelling now used by the tribe, although years ago the state legislature decided the county should be "Piute.")

Massive stone ruins of old Harrisburg, at the upper end of Quail Creek Lake.

Quail Creek State Park

Open all year
Camping, 23 units
Group camping
Picnicing
Group pavilion
Drinking water
Year-round camping; boating; fishing.

Modern restrooms, wheelchair
  accessible
Boating/fishing
Off-highway vehicles, nearby
Swimming

Historically speaking one of the newest of Utah's state parks might well have been named Harrisburg rather than Quail Creek. To be sure, the 600-acre lake does straddle upper Quail Creek which emerges from the lower slopes of the Pine Valley Mountains a dozen or so miles northeast of St. George in the southwestern corner of the state. The name of the creek apparently originated during early explorations when coveys of quail supplemented the larder of the first settlers. The birds were hunted almost to extinction and are rarely seen in this area nowadays.

The reservoir inundates one of the two sites of old Harrisburg, a thriving farming community of the period 1860-90. A few traces of the old village still stand beside the road near the park's western entrance, which is on an unnumbered road south of Leeds and east of Interstate 15.

Even when under construction in 1988, the park already was attracting upwards of 50,000 visitors a year for its excellent fishing, year-round water sports, camping, and picnicing. In addition to twenty-three campsites, some with shelters, the campground offers a fish-cleaning station, a boat ramp, and a beach.

The lake has a maximum depth of 120 feet and is cold enough to sustain rainbow trout, while largemouth bass, bluegill, and channel catfish thrive in the warmer upper levels.

Most of the lake's water supply comes not from Quail Creek but from the Virgin River through an eight-mile-long diversion tunnel. The tunnel is fed by a pipeline from a concrete dam near the town of Virgin west of Zion National Park. On top of the dam are huge steel gates (they weigh twenty tons each) that open automatically during the river's usual spring and summer freshets that sometimes become dangerous flash floods. It was those floods that washed out dam after dam when pioneer Mormon settlers tried to harness the capricious Virgin for irrigation.

Taking advantage of the rapid drop in elevation between Virgin and Quail Creek, part of the tunnel's flow has been diverted to run a hydroelectric power plant a mile and a half above the reservoir. The first of several that are planned, Plant Number One produces electricity to operate the dam and canal works, and to supply power to nearby communities. More than $800,000 a year is being realized from the sale of electricity.

Back in 1862, spring floods on Quail Creek forced the abandonment of the original site of Harrisburg. Founded two years earlier by Moses Harris and some other pioneer settlers, the settlement was relocated upstream, and it is the ruins of some of the substantial stone houses and long stone walls that lie there today, an unmarked mystery to most passersby.

Harrisburg thrived as an agricultural center, producing cotton, corn, and sorghum for the men working in the Silver Reef mines west of Leeds, which began production in 1875. But a combination of events doomed Silver Reef in the 1890s. The price of silver plummeted, the ore bodies were depleted, and a series of severe droughts and a plague of grasshoppers completed the town's decline to oblivion. Only the old Wells Fargo station stands today, restored as a shop and tourist attraction. (The remainder of the buildings were torn apart by rapacious citizens after a bag of gold was found hidden in one of the old structures.)

History does not disclose what finally became of Moses Harris, also known as Black Harris for his swarthy complexion and coal-black hair. He made his mark in history much earlier when he was a member of a notable company of adventurers, described by one of his fellow mountain men as "A free and easy kind of soul Especially with a Belly full [of liquor]."

Harris came west as a young man who was responding to an advertisement placed in the St. Louis *Missouri Gazette* on February 13, 1822, by William Henry Ashley and his partner, Andrew Henry, a miner turned mountain man. One of the most famous ads in American history, it called for "100 enterprising young men" to ascend the Missouri River to its source, "there to be employed for one, two or three years." Beaver and other furs were the main objective, and adventure was assumed since the upper Missouri and its tributaries were still mostly unknown and the tempers of the resident Indians uncertain.

Among those who replied to the advertisement or joined the company soon after were such later-to-be-famous men as Jedediah Smith, William Sublette, Thomas Fitzpatrick, Jim Bridger, Hugh Glass, and Jim Beckwourth. Later came Joe Walker, Joe Meek, Kit Carson, Old Bill Williams, and many others of the same "reckless breed of men." Such was the company that Moses Harris joined in 1822.

There appears to be no record save his own words of what he did for the next quarter of a century. He met the first of the westbound Mormon caravans near South Pass, Wyoming, in 1847. He sold the Mormons some furs and offered some discouraging news about the trail that lay ahead. Apparently he did not want any intrusion into what he regarded as his private empire. He told the Mormons that he had once traveled the entire circumference of the Great Salt Lake in 1826 and found it had no outlet. He said he was there later, in 1832, with a company of free trappers (not connected with any organization such as Ashley's). When he met the Mormon caravan, he was on his way to St. Louis to offer his services as a guide for Oregon-bound emigrants.

After that Harris vanished again from the record, and his whereabouts and activities are unknown until he helped to found Harrisburg in 1860. By that time he must have been close to sixty years old if not more, a ripe old age for any mountain man.

Numerous Indian petroglyphs of prehistoric origin on boulders near the damsite testify that Harris and his company were not the first inhabitants of the region. The big boulders were moved out of the basin before it was flooded in order to preserve those priceless records in stone.

Failure of the dike that impounded the reservoir at Quail Creek State Park in the early hours of New Year's Day 1989 caused flooding in St. George and millions of dollars in damages. The park is still open, however, and an extension of the boat ramp gives boaters access to the lake. Though smaller in acre feet than before the dike failure, the lake still provides plenty of fish for anglers.

Red Fleet State Park

Open April-November   Modern restrooms
Camping, 29 units   Sewage disposal
Picnicing   Boating/fishing
Drinking water   Swimming
Scenic red slick-rock formations; boating; camping; year-round fishing.

Utah's newest state park is also one of the most striking, with its luminous red sandstone formations towering over Red Fleet Reservoir. Named for the fancied resemblance of the formations to the sails of ships, the 650-acre reservoir was completed in 1980 as part of the giant Central Utah Project and provides culinary water to the city of Vernal and irrigation water to area farms and ranches. The park is just east of U.S. Highway 191, a few miles north of Vernal in the northeastern part of the state.

The park has sixty-one camping and picnicing sites near the lakeshore and modern restrooms without showers. A boat dock and ramp, a fish-cleaning station, a dump station, and a self-guiding nature trail are in place or in the planning stages. The lake boasts planted rainbows, largemouth bass, and a few brown trout, some of which have reached surprising size. Local boating enthusiasts liken the reservoir to its much larger cousin, Lake Powell, on the Arizona border, because of the spectacular cliffs that line the western shores of the lake.

Within the park are two dinosaur-track sites where the rocks preserve the imprint of three-toed creatures that lived here millions of years ago. One group of tracks—200 or more in number—is in the Navajo sandstone formation, which dates back about 200 million years. The tracks range in length from three to seventeen inches. The second site, in the Carmel formation, is a little more recent and has about forty tracks four to five inches in length.

Along U.S. Highway 191 from Vernal to Flaming Gorge Reservoir is a series of signs called the "Drive Through the Ages." The highway rises gradually in elevation along this route, finally topping out on a plateau at about 9,500 feet above sea level. The signs describe the various rock formations along the way as travelers successively encounter newer and newer rocks. Also nearby are Steinaker State Park and the famous Dinosaur National Monument.

Spruce trees frame anchorage at Rockport Lake.

166

Rockport State Park

Open April-November
Camping, 36 units
Group camping
Picnicing
Drinking water
Modern restrooms, wheelchair
 accessible

Vault toilets
Showers
Sewage disposal
Boating/fishing
Swimming
Cross-country skiing

Prime water recreation area; boating; swimming; camping; sailboarding; housekeeping cabins; year-round fishing.

"What's in a name?" asked Shakespeare in *Romeo and Juliet*. In the case of Rockport Lake and Wanship Dam on the Weber River thirty miles east of Salt Lake City, there is a lot of history and a bit of confusion about both names.

Wanship Dam is named for a nearby village below the dam which, more than a century and a quarter ago, was in its turn named for a friendly Indian chief. Rockport, of the same vintage, is a misspelling of Rock Fort, a pioneer settlement dating from 1860 that was inundated when the reservoir was completed.

Situated just off Interstate 80 and bordered by U.S. Highway 189, the lake is one of the state's most accessible recreation areas and is well used much of the year. By 1988 its annual visitation was estimated at 390,000.

One of two major water-storage and flood-control dams on the sometimes-turbulent Weber River, Wanship Dam was constructed in 1955-57; it is 156 feet high and 2,016 feet long at the crest. The reservoir has a capacity of 62,100 acre-feet and is an important part of the Weber Basin Project developed and maintained by the U.S. Bureau of Reclamation. Echo Reservoir, a dozen miles downstream, also is part of the project.

The State Division of Parks and Recreation assumed the management and development of the lake's recreation facilities in 1960 under a lease agreement covering 550 acres of shoreline and the lake's thousand-acre surface. Recreation facilities include thirty-six improved campsites and 200 primitive sites with pit toilets. There are three group picnic sites for day use (one subject to reservation) and three group camping areas also subject to prior reservation.

In addition, several rustic cabins are available for rental in summer adjacent to a small store that offers groceries, short-order meals, fishing and camping supplies, boat rentals, gasoline, and boat storage. There is a concrete boat-launching ramp on the east shore near the campground.

Besides camping in spring, summer, and fall, the park draws throngs for boating, fishing, sailing, water-skiing, swimming, and, in winter, ice fishing, and cross-country skiing.

Before and for a short time after the completion of the transcontinental railroad in 1869, Wanship was a busy stopping place on the Overland Stage route. As mentioned, it was called Wanship by its early settlers in appreciation for the friendship of a local Indian chief by that name, leader of a mixed band of Utes and Shoshones living in and around the Salt Lake Valley. His name was said to mean "good man," and a good man he was in maintaining peace between the settlers and more hostile elements among the other local tribes.

Originally the seat of Summit County, the town of Wanship lost out to Coalville, eight miles downstream, after the discovery of and construction of a railroad coaling station there. The first settler of record in the Wanship area was one Robert Nixon, who built a cabin at the junction of Silver Creek and the Weber River in 1859.

Rock Fort, first settled in 1860 by a man named Henry Reynolds, was originally called Three Mile Creek, presumably because it was just three miles from Wanship. Later the place was called Crandall, which name is preserved in Crandall Creek, and then Enoch, the latter a prominent name in Mormon scripture.

Indian troubles in the region in 1865 threatened the villagers, who erected a rock fort with walls eight feet high and two feet thick. Thus the settlement became known as Rock Fort, a name that somehow became translated to Rockport. Rockport it remained until construction of Wanship Dam in the 1950s inundated the village.

Scofield State Park

Mountain View

Open April-November
Camping, 34 units
Picnicing
Drinking water
Modern restrooms
Vault toilets

Showers
Sewage disposal
Boating/fishing
Off-highway vehicles, nearby
Swimming
Snowmobiling

Madsen Bay

Open April-November
Camping, 100 units
Group camping
Picnicing
Group pavilion

Vault toilets
Boating/fishing
Off-highway vehicles, nearby
Swimming
Snowmobiling

High mountain lake; camping; year-round fishing.

One of central Utah's most popular water-based playgrounds, Scofield Reservoir occupies a high, subalpine meadow called Pleasant Valley on the upper Price River, where the reservoir was created in the 1940s to impound irrigation water for farmlands along the river below.

At an elevation of 7,600 feet above sea level, the lake is the location of Utah's highest state park, plus a sprawling community of summer homes and trailer camps. Both the reservoir and the state park are named for the old mining town of Scofield, a short way above the lake. Scofield was the site of the state's first commercial coal mines, where in 1900 there occurred one of the worst mine disasters in United States history.

Scofield State Park comprises 312 acres of land leased since 1963 from the federal Bureau of Reclamation on the eastern shore of the 2,800-acre lake. The Mountain View camping area has two boat-launching ramps. The park is officially closed in winter, but the lake is open for fishing all year, including ice fishing in winter. Snowmobiling is another popular winter sport. The cool waters are considered ideal for trout, and the reservoir is stocked with rain-

Some of the summer homes on the shore of Scofield Lake.

Miners who dug graves for victims of 1900 mine disaster at Scofield.

bow by the Utah State Division of Wildlife Resources. Native cutthroat trout also inhabit the lake and the streams that flow into it.

In summer, Scofield Reservoir attracts throngs of campers, fishermen, and boating enthusiasts, although the water is too cold for most scuba divers and swimmers. The park campground is often full to capacity in the summer, bringing the annual visitor total to more than 230,000, not counting visitors to the lake outside the park boundaries.

The town of Scofield was named for General Charles W. Scofield, a timber contractor in the area after the Civil War. He became president of the first coal-mining company when it was organized by eastern interests. The town, which reached its peak of population about 1920, was originally called Pleasant Valley when settlement began in the 1870s.

Nothing about the lake or the park except the name of Scofield serves to remind anyone now of the terrible event of May 1, 1900. On that day in the Winter Quarters coal mine, a gas explosion took 199 lives, the vast majority recent immigrants from Finland, Italy, and other countries. The bodies of 149 of the victims still lie in Scofield cemetery, a registered National Historic Site.

In terms of loss of life, the disaster was the nation's worst mining accident on record up to that time, and it resulted in widespread public demand for better mine safety. President McKinley telegraphed his condolences to the families of the victims, a year before he fell victim to an assassin's bullet. President Loubet of France sent a message of sympathy. The mines reopened several months later, although many of the surviving miners refused to work there and moved away.

With the decline in the world demand for coal due in part to the advent of diesel-powered locomotives and the growing use of natural gas in homes and industry, many of the coal mines in the region have closed, and the town of Scofield has dwindled to a few hundred inhabitants. Today the remaining coal mines of Carbon County provide fuel for industry and for Utah power plants that send electricity as far as Los Angeles.

State Route 96 continues south past the Scofield townsite to a junction with State Route 264, which, a few miles to the west, connects with Utah's scenic Skyline Drive along the crest of the Wasatch Plateau.

Typical rock formation in Snow Canyon.

172

Snow Canyon State Park

Open all year	Modern restrooms, wheelchair
Camping, 34 units	accessible
Group camping	Vault toilets
Picnicking	Sewage disposal
Group pavilion	Utility hookups, electricity only
Drinking water	Concessionaire

Moderate climate allows early spring outings; camping; hiking; photography.

Any misguided winter sports enthusiast who might trek to Snow Canyon State Park for the skiing or bobsledding would be in for a considerable shock. Snow Canyon is named not for any abundance of the white powdery stuff, but for two pioneer Mormons — Apostles Lorenzo and Erastus Snow — who helped to settle this part of southwestern Utah in the early 1860s.

From a climatic point of view, the park's original name, Dixie State Park, would seem more appropriate, since the park is situated in the region known as Utah's Dixie, formerly a cotton-growing region that boasts the lowest elevation in the state. Dixie is noted for its long, hot summers and brief, mild winters, and is becoming increasingly popular as a retirement community.

Snow Canyon lies 3,400 feet above sea level. Neighboring St. George, largest city in southern Utah, sprawls beside Interstate 15 at 2,900 feet, while nearby residential Bloomington is only 2,600 feet above sea level. For a Rocky Mountain state, that is low down.

At any altitude, however, Snow Canyon would be a remarkable place. If the name Kodachrome Basin had not already been applied to another highly colorful state park farther east, it would be well suited to Snow Canyon, which quite literally beggars description.

Three miles long and nearly a thousand feet deep, Snow Canyon in simple terms is a flat-bottomed gorge slashed by erosion through brilliant pink, red, and yellow sandstone that is mantled by great masses of black lava. Eons of weathering have carved the

173

sandstone into an endless variety of forms that delight artists and photographers as well as geologists and rock climbers. There are formations like frosted cupcakes, domes and cones that pierce the sky, layered and fluted cliffs like heaps of taffy candy, sharp angles and crevices formed by vertical fractures, and extraordinary abstract patterns caused by crossbedding in the sedimentary strata.

Geologists estimate the age of the sandstone layers at some three million years (the Triassic period), in contrast to the far more recent lava flows, the last of which may have occurred as little as a thousand years ago. The main source of the lava appears to have been a vent that now may be seen as a perfectly formed volcanic cone at the canyon's northeastern end, just off State Route 18. There is a foot trail to the summit.

Now covering 6,800 acres, the park property was acquired between 1959 and 1964 from Washington County and from several private owners, partly by gift and partly by purchase. There was little development until 1970, but since then complete public facilities have been installed including paved roads, several covered RV shelters with electrical hookups, and picnic and playground areas. Visitor totals approach 230,000 a year, heaviest in spring and fall but running around 10,000 to 12,000 a month even during summer.

Under its original name of Dixie State Park, the park included two historic homes—the winter home of Brigham Young in St. George and the Jacob Hamblin home in Santa Clara between St. George and the present park. Both buildings were acquired from private owners by the Utah Division of Parks and Recreation, restored to their original appearance and appropriately furnished, then turned over to the Mormon church early in the 1970s. In return, the church deeded to the state the Brigham Young Forest Farmhouse in Salt Lake City, which was then relocated to Pioneer Trail State Park.

After directing that the Dixie region be settled in 1861 as part of the growing Mormon empire, Brigham Young spent the winter of 1870-71 there, finding the mild winter climate better suited to his advancing years than Salt Lake City. He returned there a year later to dedicate the site for a temple, and thereafter spent a few months there each winter except for 1875-76. During his final visit in 1877 he dedicated the completed temple. He died in Salt Lake City in August of that year.

By the 1940s the old home had been abandoned and was in a sorry state of repair. Through the cooperation of the Brigham Young Memorial Foundation it was taken over by the state and completely refurbished in its original elaborate mid-Victorian style. It is open all year for public tours.

Jacob Hamblin, one of the most famous of Utah's Mormon pioneers, came to Santa Clara in 1854 along with a small group of settlers who built cabins and irrigation works and planted cotton, fruit trees, grapes, and other crops. They also built a rock fort for protection against Indians. Hamblin built his two-story rock home in 1862 and remained there until he moved to Kanab in 1870.

His home, an outstanding example of frugal frontier architecture, is built of rough-hewn native sandstone and roofed with hand-split cedar shingles. After Hamblin moved away, the building was occupied off and on until it was abandoned in 1959. It was then given by the Hamblin family to the state, which undertook its complete restoration. Like the Brigham Young home, it is open daily for public visits.

After settling in Arizona in 1878, Hamblin died in 1886 while on a visit to New Mexico. He had become widely known not only for his peacemaking efforts with the Indians of the region, but for his trailbreaking work as a guide and advisor for various government surveys in Utah and Arizona.

Among other exploits, he visited the Hopi villages of Arizona as a missionary, having crossed the Colorado River at the Crossing of the Fathers, probably the first European to have done so in the seventy-five years since Escalante and Dominguez. He also made the first successful crossing of the Colorado at the mouth of the Paria River, at a place later to be known as Lee's Ferry, now in Arizona.

Joshua forest along old U.S. Highway 91 east of St. George.

176

Joshua Trees—Utah's Improbable Lilies*

Although Joshua trees are scattered along Interstate 15 and elsewhere around St. George, most travelers speeding along that busy freeway probably do not recognize them as giant yuccas, largest native members of the lily family.

Brigham Young is credited with naming these grotesque, oversized plants Joshua trees, likening their haphazard branches to the arms of the Biblical prophet frantically waving in the wilderness.

Between Littlefield, Arizona, twenty-five miles south of St. George, and the Beaver Dam Mountains in the extreme southwestern corner of Utah, Joshuas occur by the uncounted thousands along old U.S. Highway 91, a marginally maintained route that connects with State Route 18 at Veyo, north of Snow Canyon State Park.

The vast forest of giant yuccas shows up on some road maps as a "point of interest," but no roadside marker mentions them. A spectacular sight when they burst into bloom, usually in late spring at intervals of two or three years, their large, creamy-white, nectar-laden blossoms attract swarms of birds and insects.

The Joshua tree also occurs in large forests in Arizona, Nevada, and California as well as in Utah. One area of 1,344 square miles in southeastern California has been set aside as Joshua Tree National Monument, and other smaller groves are preserved in other parks in the Southwest.

Not really a tree in the technical sense, since it is actually a hollow bundle of fibers, the Joshua has no annual rings by which its age might be determined. As a species, it is believed to be extremely ancient. It probably dates from at least the Tertiary period, which lasted sixty million years ago to about one million years ago. Its remains have been found in association with those of the long-extinct tree sloth, which evidently made its diet almost exclusively of its leaves.

---

*Portions of this essay appeared in the Sunday Travel Section of the *New York Times* of June 22, 1969, and are used by permission.

When it is not in bloom, the Joshua presents a decidedly hostile appearance, repelling to some viewers but a safe haven for desert dwellers small enough to take shelter within its spiny covering. The tiny desert lizard called Xantusia lives out its entire life in the Joshua tree, which also is a favorite habitat for desert wrens, flickers, woodpeckers, bluebirds, owls, orioles, and flycatchers. Pack rats gather the spiny leaves for their untidy nests. Botanically speaking, however, the Joshua behaves much like other members of the widespread tribe of yuccas.

The yuccas have many names. In addition to Joshua trees, some varieties are known as tree yuccas, yucca palms, soapweed, Adam's Needle, Spanish dagger, Spanish bayonet, wild date (from the shape of its fruit), and Lord's Candle, the last referring to the tall, white plumes made up of thousands of individual waxy blossoms.

Because the yuccas are some of the most prominent and best known of southwestern desert plants, it seems only proper that ranger-naturalists in state and national parks and monuments in several western states should make it the subject of summer fireside talks and slide shows. The yucca story is a favorite with naturalists everywhere because it so strikingly illustrates the phenomenon known as *obligate symbiosis*, the life-and-death interrelationship of two utterly different life forms that has developed through evolution. The natural world is full of examples of such relationships (see essay on the lichens), but none is stranger than the weird and wonderful love affair carried on by the yucca plant and an insignificant moth.

Innumerable species of plants have always been dependent upon insects of many varieties to spread their pollen. In turn, the insects could not survive without the nectar contributed by the plant. But in most cases, the relationship apparently is random — any old Tom, Dick, or hairy insect of either sex can be responsible for the accidental fertilizing of almost any flowering plant it happens to encounter.

With the yucca and the yucca moth, things are mortally different.

Only the species of moth called Pronuba, and only the female of the species, can fertilize the yucca. And only the yucca can play foster parent to the offspring of the moth. All but one of the thirty-odd species of yuccas in the world — half of them in the

United States — are wholly dependent upon the Pronuba moth, a tiny silver-gray creature that would not rate a second glance for any other reason.

The Pronuba moth is necessarily nocturnal, since most yuccas bloom at night. Furthermore, the moth is highly developed for its special purpose. Its mouth parts are shaped to hold a ball of pollen that it gathers from the flower, in addition to the pollen that rubs off on its wings.

After visiting one shining white yucca flower, the moth carries its load of pollen to the next flower, where it assiduously jams the ball of yellow powder into the stigma, the female receptive organ of the flower. The process is not casual — the insect actually pounds the pollen into the receptacle with its head. Having thus paid her admission, the moth delves farther into the flower to deposit her eggs in the plant's ovary, where the hatching larvae are assured of an ample food supply as the seeds develop.

The timing of the whole process has to be exquisitely precise or the system will not work at all. The ovary is so small that there is barely room for the moth's eggs. If the eggs were to hatch too early, they and the seed pod would rupture and die. But the pods grow faster than the larvae, so there is room for both the swarm of tiny boarders as they hatch, develop, and grow, and for the ripening seeds that they feed upon.

Almost any ripened yucca pod will have all but a few of its thousands of tiny, black, watermelon-like seeds neatly drilled through, as though for stringing a necklace, where the larvae have eaten their way to freedom. The perforated seeds cannot sprout, but somehow the larvae "know" enough not to perforate all of them. They always leave enough whole seeds to perpetuate the species — and the future of their own race.

Since yuccas grow mostly in arid regions, water scarcity dictates that most plants grow wide apart. It goes without saying that if all the tens of thousands of seeds in the pods of a single yucca were to sprout, probably none of the youngsters would get enough water to survive. The thinning-out process performed by the larvae is ultimately as beneficial to the plant as the pollenizing.

When the yucca pod starts to wither and becomes unpalatable, the larvae arrive in the outer world through their minuscule tunnels and drop to the ground. Each is curled into a tiny ball which can roll into a safe crevice, if a bird or small animal does not get to it

Dried stalks of yucca plants in White Sands National Monument.

first. Underground, the larvae lapse into the pupal stage to wait out the cycle of the seasons.

In the following year, when the yuccas once more put up their tall flower stalks and their showers of white blossoms, it is time for the moths to break out of their underground cocoons to emerge as winged insects and start the cycle all over again. If they emerge too soon, the flowers will not be ready for them, and they will die. If they appear too late, the flowers will have withered.

This seemingly miraculous relationship of plant and insect was unknown until about a century ago, when the yucca was first introduced into the famous London Botanical Garden by plant collectors. There the plants seemed to thrive for a time but did not reproduce. Only when the Pronuba moth was discovered and introduced to the gardens did fruit develop and seeds sprout.

When the Pronuba moth is wiped out by insecticides—as has happened in some places—the yuccas eventually vanish from the region. In addition to the moth, a large butterfly species lives on the yucca, its larvae burrowing into the roots, but what, if any, benefit the plant may derive from that species is not known.

When the first Europeans arrived on this continent, they quickly found commercial uses for the yucca and threatened to destroy the plants in certain areas. The wood was used to fire boilers at early western mines, a jute substitute was made from its fibers, and in World War I some newspapers were printed on paper made from yucca pulp.

Indians of the Southwest knew a great deal about the yucca plant and its manifold uses, too. Some tribes ate the buds, flowers, young stalks, and seeds, and still do on occasion. They pounded the fleshy leaves to a pulp, from which they extracted long, tough fibers for ropes, twine, matting, nets, hairbrushes, hats, basketry, and a kind of coarse cloth. They used the hard, dead stalks for everything from house building to weapons, from ribs for canoes to ceremonial wands. It is no wonder the plant and its pollen are still regarded as sacred by many.

Starvation State Park

Open all year	Vault toilets
Camping, 31 units	Showers
Group camping	Sewage disposal
Picnicing	Boating/fishing
Drinking water	Off-highway vehicles, nearby
Modern restrooms, wheelchair	Swimming
accessible	Concessionaire

3,310 surface-acre lake boating; camping; year-round fishing.

A name grim as Starvation State Park implies a notable tragedy at some earlier date, although published histories of the area do not mention one. Local legend offers two conflicting tales.

One version says a group of fur trappers caught in the area long ago by winter snows survived by stealing food cached by the local Indians, leaving the Indians to starve. The opposite (and more commonly told) version says it was the Indians who stole the trappers' food, leaving them to starve. Precisely who starved and when remains a mystery, although an estimate of the time may be made from the fact that fur trapping pretty much ceased after about 1840. The cache—whomever it belonged to—was supposedly in a group of caves and rocky holes along the southwest shore of the reservoir.

Starvation State Park, formerly Starvation Lake State Recreation Area, was established in 1972 to administer public recreation on the lake and develop picnic, camping, and boating facilities near the dam on the southeast side of the lake. The park's land area totals 3,445 acres. The main campground has a large concrete boat-launching ramp adjacent to a boat-trailer parking yard and a beach-picnic area.

The park is especially popular on weekends, and while camping spaces are usually available during the week, advance reservations are advisable on summer weekends and midseason holidays. There are also two big overflow camping areas on arms of the lake and some day-use access points along the lake shore for fishermen.

Starvation Dam and Reservoir were begun in 1970 by the U.S.

Bureau of Reclamation as part of the Central Utah Project's
Bonneville Unit, and they are operated for conservation and flood
control by the Central Utah Water Conservancy District. The dam
is 2,920 feet long and 200 feet high, storing a maximum of
167,310 acre feet of water supplied by the Strawberry River and
smaller creeks. The spillway elevation is 5,700 feet.

The park's entrance station is four miles west of the town of
Duchesne off U.S. Highway 40, which crosses the southwestern
arm of the lake at a point called the Dominguez-Escalante Overlook. At this spot stands one of several highway markers erected in
1976 at various sites to commemorate the bicentennial of a
momentous adventure—the exploration of much of what is now
Utah by two Spanish missionary priests and their handful of
followers seventy years before the Mormon occupation. The names
of many geographical landmarks in New Mexico, Colorado, Utah,
and Arizona originated on that trip.

Seeking a direct way west to the newly established mission and
presidio of Monterey that would avoid the barrier of the Grand
Canyon and the scorching deserts of more southern routes, and
eager to explore new areas that might offer potential converts and
allies, the expedition left Santa Fe on July 29, 1776. It was supposed to leave on July 4 but was delayed by pressing local affairs.
Certainly none of the party had any remote idea of what was
happening in Philadelphia at that precise time in history, any more
than the signers of the Declaration of Independence knew what
was afoot in the Spanish Southwest.

The leaders of the Spanish expedition were Fray Francisco
Atanasio Dominguez, superior of the New Mexico Franciscans,
and Fray Silvestre Vélez de Escalante of Zuni, a diligent diarist.
Sharing the task of leading the expedition was one Don Bernardo
Miera y Pacheco, engineer, retired military captain, and cartogra-
pher. He was the custodian of the astrolabe, a primitive instrument
for measuring the elevation of celestial bodies to estimate latitude
but not longitude. The astrolabe could tell them how far north
they had come and how far south they had to go to get home, but
nothing about their east-west orientation. That was a job for a
sextant and chronometer, neither of which they had. They did have
three Indian guides for various sections of their journey.

From Santa Fe, the ten men and a group of cattle brought
along as beefsteak-on-the-hoof traveled north through northern

New Mexico and southern Colorado for twenty days, stopping the night of August 17 near the Utah-Colorado border. They then turned northeastward, still in familiar territory, for earlier Spanish explorers and trappers and traders had ventured northward a decade or so earlier, probably as far as the Dolores and Gunnison rivers and the Uncompahgre Plateau. One member of the party, Andres Muñiz, knew something of the language of the "Yutas" and had previously traveled as far as the Gunnison. On the North Fork of the Gunnison, the band recruited two Utes of the "Timpangotzis" band, who guided them westward. Crossing into what is now Utah not far from the dinosaur quarry in the southwestern corner of Dinosaur National Monument, they left an inscription on a tree by the side of the Green River at a site now marked by a monument, although the tree is long gone.

It was on this leg of the journey that they followed and crossed a small stream (the Strawberry River) on September 19 after struggling through deep ravines and brush-filled gullies now flooded by Starvation Lake. As Escalante's diary relates, "We descended to the river, making several turns through almost impassable terrain, now through many stones, now along rocky precipices. One of them caused one of our horses to be injured, and made us backtrack about a mile and descend to another meadow of the river. We crossed it by breaking though a bosque of osier, and tall bamboo reed, and at half a league swung for the northwest by taking the channel bed of an arroyo for our route, ascending the sierra and leaving the Strawberry [River] behind." The party finally left the canyon through Rabbit Gulch (directly across the lake north of the highway bridge) and proceeded more or less due west along the Diamond Fork and Spanish Fork rivers to the shores of Utah Lake just south of present-day Provo, where they found a village of shy but friendly Ute Indians.

After spending three days resting and feasting on shellfish supplied by the Indians, the party proceeded southwest, ignoring descriptions of a "great salt lake" off to the north. There was some speculation among the men that the salt water might even be an arm of the Pacific Ocean. Rife with dissension over whether to continue westward or return to Santa Fe in the face of gathering snowstorms, the party prayed and cast lots while in camp on the Beaver River, a little west of present-day Minersville, on October 11 (see Minersville State Park).

Sailboats ashore beside picnic area at Starvation State Park.

The lots told them to go home. Their return route took them south across the Virgin River above present-day St. George, then eastward to find the difficult crossing of the Colorado River (the Crossing of the Fathers) in Glen Canyon, at a point now below the waters of Lake Powell. From there they trekked south and east through territory more or less familiar to the expedition's leaders — familiar, but not easy, since winter was upon them and many of the Indians along the way were not helpful.

Ragged, gaunt, and worn to the bone, the adventurers arrived back in Santa Fe on January 2, 1777, after stopping at various Spanish missions along the homeward route. They had covered 1,700 miles of largely unknown territory in a little more than five months without losing a man or firing a shot in anger. It was to be another half century before American and French-Canadian fur trappers would arrive on the scene to end Utah's isolation forever (*see* Hyrum, Green River, and Fort Buenaventura state parks for more on the fur trade), and yet another two decades before Mormon colonizing finally brought European-style civilization to that wild frontier.

Steinaker State Park

Open April-November
Camping, 31 units
Picnicing
Group pavilion
Drinking water

Modern restrooms, wheelchair
  accessible
Sewage disposal
Boating/fishing
Off-highway vehicles, nearby
Swimming

Camping area for Dinosaurland; boating; water-skiing; year-round fishing.

Steinaker State Park's convenient location seven miles north of Vernal off U.S. Highway 191 makes it a popular base for exploring the many attractions of Dinosaurland in northeast Utah (*see* Utah Field House of Natural History). It is also a convenient night camping place for travelers to and from Flaming Gorge National Recreation Area, thirty-odd miles to the north.

At an altitude of 5,400 feet, tree-lined Steinaker Lake is popular all summer as a visitor's base camp and as a vacation spot for campers, picnicers, swimmers, and sunbathers. Summer weekends and holidays often find the campground full. In midsummer the lake's water temperature often exceeds 70 degrees at the surface. But at the dam, where it is 162 feet deep, the lake is cool enough to support not only bluegill and largemouth bass, but also rainbow trout. Winter fishing through the ice is permitted.

In 1961, the ground-breaking ceremonies for the dam were attended by the man for whom the lake and the park are named. He was John Steinaker, member of a pioneer ranching family in the region and eighty-one years of age at the time. Principal speaker at the ceremony was Fred G. Aandahl, Assistant Secretary of the Interior, who was presented with a "Dinosaur Hunting License" and a bronzed miniature of the region's dinosaur mascot. Also speaking was an assistant to the Secretary of the Interior, former Utah Senator Arthur V. Watkins, for whom Watkins Dam at Willard Bay is named (*see* Willard Bay State Park).

Steinaker Lake itself is an unusual water-storage facility. It is supplied by a canal from a diversion dam on Ashley Creek several

Camping at Steinaker Lake among sagebrush-covered hills.

miles to the west. One of the first units to be constructed in the vast Central Utah Project, Steinaker Lake stores runoff water from Ashley Creek to provide supplementary irrigation for 15,000 acres in Ashley Valley. When it is full, Steinaker Lake covers 750 surface acres with a maximum storage capacity of 38,100 acre feet of water. Ashley Creek and Ashley Valley are named for General William H. Ashley, famous for his leadership in the fur trade in the West in the 1820s and 1830s (*see* the essay The Naming and Taming of the Green).

In addition to its obvious attractions for water recreation, Steinaker Lake is in a region well known to geologists, historians, and collectors of artifacts. Fossilized relics of ancient seas such as oysters, clams, and other shellfish are found here, and on the adjacent hills obsidian chips and arrowheads turn up from time to time. Bone beads ascribed to the early Basketmaker culture occur on some of the sand ridges, and in caves to the north Basketmaker burial sites have been discovered.

Territorial Statehouse State Park, Fillmore, Utah.

Original architect's sketch of proposed territorial statehouse at Fillmore, Utah.

188

Territorial Statehouse State Park

Open all year   Museum
Day-use only   Drinking water
Picnicing   Modern restrooms
Museum; pioneer and Indian artifacts.

The vast territory of Utah in 1851 covered nearly four times its present area when Governor Brigham Young proclaimed the town-to-be of Fillmore, 140 miles south of Salt Lake City, as the territorial capital and ordered the construction of a large and ornate capitol building.

At the time, Utah sprawled over some 320,000 square miles of thinly populated Rocky Mountain, Great Basin, and desert terrain, including most of what is now Nevada and western Colorado. Governor Young selected the site because it was close to the geographic center of the territory, though far from other settlements.

Having petitioned Washington for Utah statehood, he envisioned the infant city as the state (rather than the territorial) seat of government and named it Fillmore after Millard Fillmore, who served as president of the United States from 1850 to 1853. The county became Millard County.

But, for a variety of reasons both political and geographical, Brigham Young's dream did not come true. Utah did not achieve statehood until 1896, and in the interim the territory fell victim to what its citizens considered a series of large-scale land grabs. All of what is now Nevada except for its southern tip was carved out of Utah Territory in 1861, 1862, and 1866; Colorado took another big chunk in 1861; and Wyoming received a small area in 1868. The remaining 84,990 square miles rank Utah today as the eleventh largest state, instead of second, as it might have been.

And instead of the fabulous Arabian Nights dream of a great capitol building, only the south wing of the proposed structure was ever even started. Even after completion, the territorial legislature met there only three times: in December 1855; a year later, but just long enough to adjourn to Salt Lake City; and finally in

1868 when the delegates voted to move the capital permanently to Salt Lake City.

Had it ever been completed, the capitol complex at Fillmore would have consisted of four wings in the form of a cross dominated by a great Moorish-style dome rising in the center. The architect was Truman O. Angell, credited with the design of the celebrated Mormon Tabernacle in Salt Lake City.

The handsome red sandstone statehouse and its half acre of land were acquired by the State Division of Parks and Recreation in 1957 after the building was rescued by the Daughters of Utah Pioneers from decades of neglect. The DUP took it over from the state in 1930 and restored it. Previously the building had served briefly as a newspaper printing plant, a civic center, a church, a school, a jail, and a theater, all before 1900.

Now completely renovated, the statehouse is a model museum, with two floors and a basement full of well-displayed and well-cataloged pictures and memorabilia from the late nineteenth and early twentieth centuries, much donated by residents of the area. Early firearms, farming equipment, and woodworking tools, butter churns, clothes washers, handmade furniture, glassware, and dishes are on display.

Also included are many artifacts from the local Paiute Indians, whose Chief Kanosh, a lifelong friend of the Mormon settlers, joined the church in his later years. When he died in 1881, the old chief was given a Mormon funeral and was buried in the Christian cemetery in the nearby village named for him.

The town of Fillmore, commercial center and seat of Millard County, now has a population of about 2,000, the largest town between Nephi and Cedar City. In addition to the old statehouse, it has several other buildings listed on the National Historic Register, including a rock schoolhouse built in 1867.

The town is surrounded by volcanic outcroppings, some of them fairly recent, most notably the Millard Volcanic Field west of the interstate highway, a large area of lava formations, extinct craters, hot springs, and ice caves.

Visitor totals now exceed 22,000 annually. The park is open all year during daylight hours.

Utah Field House of Natural History State Park

Open all year   Museum
Day-use only   Drinking water
Picnicing   Modern restrooms
Natural history museum; thirteen life-size dinosaur replicas; skeletal reproductions; fluorescent mineral display.

It might be possible to slip through Vernal in northeastern Utah without meeting a dinosaur, but you would have to do it in a hurry and in the middle of the night, hoping all the critters would be asleep or looking the other way.

Crazy? Not entirely, because Vernal is the permanent home of more dinosaurs than any other town anywhere, ever. And of course they never sleep since they are all made of fiber glass.

Fourteen life-size replicas of dinosaurs and other prehistoric animals occupy a pleasant, tree-shaded garden on U.S. Highway 40, Vernal's main street, adjacent to the Utah Field House of Natural History, a handsome brick museum building which is also the local state park headquarters and visitor center. Locally called Dinosaur Gardens, the state park should not be confused with Dinosaur National Monument, which straddles the Utah-Colorado border farther east, nor with the world-famous dinosaur quarry north of Jensen on the western edge of the national monument.

Regional capital of northeastern Utah and seat of Uintah County, bustling Vernal is at the junction of several state highways with Highway 40 and is on the main route to Flaming Gorge National Recreation Area on the Utah-Wyoming border.

The Field House Museum has a large assortment of specimens in anthropology, natural history, geology, and paleontology. There are relics of prehistoric and recent Indian residents of the region, fine mineral exhibits, plants and wildlife, fossils, models, and reconstructed skeletons of long-vanished species. Paintings of ancient landscapes and life forms from the area are also on display.

During the summer, approximately from Memorial Day to Labor Day, the Field House is open from 8 A.M. to 9 P.M. During

191

the winter months the museum and gardens are open from 9 A.M. to 5 P.M. The park is closed on Thanksgiving Day, Christmas Day, and New Year's Day. Visitation now totals nearly 200,000 a year.

The museum was established by the state legislature in 1945 and opened to the public in 1948. Since 1959 it has been administered by the State Division of Parks and Recreation. The adjacent Dinosaur Gardens were added to the park in 1978. In preparation for the addition, the city had to remove a municipal swimming pool as well as some monuments and trees. After the monsters were in place, more trees and shrubs were planted, a pond was built in the center, and foot trails were provided for strolls through the gardens.

The fourteen models of prehistoric animals in the park are the creation of Elbert H. Porter, a professional artist with a master's degree from the University of Utah, where he taught sculpture for twelve years. Inspired by a visit to Dinosaur National Monument in 1958, Porter and his wife traveled across the country studying exhibits of dinosaur fossils and reproductions in museums and universities before undertaking small-scale (one-twelfth life-size) construction of the animals.

From these experimental models, Porter perfected his technique for making full-size creatures from fiber glass molded over plywood frames, a long and tedious process that took as much as a year for some of the larger ones. All in all, the animals in the Dinosaur Gardens represent fourteen years of labor.

After the dinosaurs were finished, the Porters displayed some of them at the family's studio in Draper, south of Salt Lake City. Then they were displayed in West Yellowstone, Montana, as a tourist attraction, and finally settled down at Orderville, east of Zion National Park. There the creatures remained until they were acquired by the State Division of Parks and Recreation in 1977.

The animals now residing in the Dinosaur Gardens include the horned Triceratops, which weighed seven or eight tons; the six-ton Stegosaurus, which had a brain no larger than a kitten's; the enormous plant-eating Diplodocus, more than eighty feet long and weighing twelve tons; and the winged Pteranodon, one of the largest flying creatures ever, with a wingspan of twenty-five feet or more.

Then there is Edaphosaurus, a fin-backed reptile from Texas

Dinosaur Gardens, Utah Field House of Natural History State Park.

that you would not want to meet in a dark alley, and the birdlike Ornithomimus, twelve feet long and seven feet high. Towering over the garden paths, its dagger-like six-inch teeth bared, stands Tyrannosaurus Rex, literally king of the dinosaurs, largest of all the meat-eaters. Up to fifty feet in length and eighteen to twenty feet tall, it weighed an estimated eight tons. Off in a corner, dwarfed by some of the others, stands a woolly mammoth fourteen feet high at the shoulder, with huge, curving tusks.

Dinosaurs are by no means the only attractions in and around Vernal, which is situated at the center of a wide web of both man-made and natural wonders. The Vernal Chamber of Commerce issues a series of eight brochures that provide clear mile-by-mile directions for one-day tours to such points of interest as Flaming Gorge, Red Fleet Reservoir, Browns Park on the upper Green River, and the Ute Indian Tribe's resort and recreational site at Bottle Hollow Reservoir.

There is also a brochure describing a "Drive Through the Ages," an auto tour north of Vernal on which one can see at close range geological formations representing untold millions of years of the earth's history. Another brochure gives details of a forty-minute walking tour of Vernal with its museums, city parks, churches, and a bank built of bricks mailed to the site by parcel post because it was cheaper than rail freight.

Utah Lake State Park

Open all year
Camping
Picnicing
Visitor center/museum
Drinking water

Modern restrooms, wheelchair
  accessible
Showers
Sewage disposal
Boating/fishing
Swimming

Major access to 96,600 acre freshwater lake; boating; camping; picnicking; ice skating; year-round fishing.

There is so much to see and do in and around Provo (named after early mountain man Etienne Provost) that it would be easy for a visitor to overlook the many and varied activities at Utah Lake State Park, four miles west of the city's center on the east shore of Utah Lake.

The lake itself has a long and not always happy history dating from the Dominguez-Escalante expedition, which spent several days there in 1776 (*see* Starvation State Park). Once subject to extreme fluctuations in depth from both natural and man-made causes, sometimes at flood stage, sometimes almost a mudhole, Utah Lake is now stabilized at about 150 square miles of surface area, making it Utah's largest natural body of fresh water. Principal access to the lake is at the state park, where year-round camping is permitted on a no-reservation basis. Dedicated in 1967, the park comprises 300 acres. It has 120 developed camping spaces with picnic tables, barbecue grills, modern restrooms with showers, and a sewage dump station. A thirty-acre marina has 144 boat spaces, four concrete boat-launching ramps, and boat and trailer storage.

An unusual and highly popular feature of the state park is its Olympic-size skating rink, primarily used for winter skating on artificial ice but converted to roller skating all summer. A small fee is charged for admission and for rental of skates.

The Provo River, flowing past the park into the lake, and the Jordan River (*see* Jordan River State Park), the lake's outlet, are both popular for canoeing, kayaking, and fishing. The lake offers good fishing for carp, catfish, and yellow perch, and has produced some record-size bass (four pounds, one ounce), black bullhead (two pounds, seven ounces), and walleye (twelve pounds, eleven ounces). As late as 1864, huge commercial catches of trout were being made on the lake, but within a few years the trout had all disappeared and many other species were nearly exhausted as well. In modern times, however, a few commercial seiners continue to net nongame fish for retail marketing.

Beginning in the late 1870s, heavy diversion of the lake's water through the Jordan River and a system of canals led to heated disputes over water rights between farmers and industrialists that continued for nearly a century. Only the intervention of Mormon church officials averted what might have become a shooting war. At one point, pumping for irrigation and industrial use during a drought lowered the lake level to less than a foot of water in places and nearly all the remaining fish died.

Since the 1970s, however, both Utah Lake and the Jordan River have become multipurpose recreational facilities, and the lake level usually does not change much, though it did rise considerably during the high-water period of the mid-1980s, when much of the state park was flooded.

Because the lake's depth averages only about ten feet, wave action keeps mineral deposits churned up to such an extent that the water is never really clear, but it is nonetheless good for swimming and water-skiing as well as wind surfing, boating, and fishing. During times of storms and high winds, or when it is frozen over, the lake is closed to such activities.

Historically, the lake at one time was the region's most productive fishery. Fray Escalante said in his diary in September 1776 that the friendly local Indians were known as the Fish Eaters. Escalante called the lake Timpanogotizis, about as close as his Spanish language could come to the native's own pronunciation. The map maker Miera wrote, "Laguna de los Timpangos" on his remarkable map of the Great Basin, and eventually the name settled at Timpanogos, which is applied to a cave and national monument, a mountain peak, and a scenic canyon, all in close proximity.

Cascade Springs, Wasatch Mountain State Park.

196

Wasatch Mountain State Park

Open all year	Showers
Camping, 152 units	Sewage disposal
Group camping	Utility hookups
Picnicing	Golfing
Group pavilion	Off-road vehicles, nearby
Visitor center/museum	Snowmobiling
Drinking water	Cross-country skiing
Modern restrooms, wheelchair accessible	Concessionaire

Summer camping; picnicing; hiking; twenty-seven-hole golf course; winter snowmobiling; cross-country skiing.

One of the oldest, largest, and best developed of Utah's state parks, Wasatch Mountain enjoys the distinction of being the only state park in Utah (if not the nation) with its own railroad (*see* the Heber Creeper Story at the end of this article). It is also known for its highly diverse year-round scenic and recreational attractions, including a challenging twenty-seven-hole golf course.

On property acquired in 1961 for $1.54 million, the park spreads over 22,000 acres of wooded mountain and valley landscape on the eastern slope of the Wasatch Range about thirty-five miles southeast of Salt Lake City and six miles west of U.S. Highway 40 at Heber City. State Route 224 (closed in winter) roughly bisects the park, running north from Midway to Park City. Another road (State Route 190), this one gravel, branches off to the west, switchbacks over the Wasatch Range, and ends up at the Brighton Ski Resort in Big Cottonwood Canyon. It, too, is closed in winter.

The park's elevation of 5,775 feet above sea level (at the visitor center) assures it ample snow for winter sports—from three to six feet most winters, when nighttime temperatures below zero are to be expected. Although there are no ski lifts in the park itself, snowmobile trails lead into the nearby mountains, and cross-country skiing is very popular on the golf course.

The bulk of Wasatch Mountain's visitors, totaling close to

80,000 a year, arrive in spring, summer, and fall. Camping, picnicing, horseback riding on established trails, and fishing and
hunting in the vicinity are among the park's many activities in
addition to golf.

One portion of the park on the southern edge of the village of
Midway centers around a large, rustic building called the Chalet.
Available by advance reservation for group parties, family outings,
and business meetings, the facility has restrooms, tables, and
chairs. Tableware may be rented. A picnic area, horseshoe pits, a
softball diamond, and volleyball courts adjoin the Chalet.

The park's big Pine Creek Campground, north of the golf
course, has 152 developed spaces providing individual water, electricity, and sewer hookups, plus a tent area, a pavilion, and an
amphitheater. There are modern restrooms with showers and an
RV dump station. A primitive campground on upper Deer Creek
is much used by scouting, church, and family groups.

Although not actually part of Wasatch Mountain State Park,
the incredibly beautiful mountain retreat known as Cascade
Springs in the Uinta National Forest shares a common boundary
with the park. At Cascade Springs, an odd geological formation
enables warm ground water to surge to the surface down a lush,
mossy hillside some 6,300 feet above sea level, six miles southwest
of Midway. A wide variety of trees, shrubs, flowers, ferns, and
vines borders a series of natural terraces that resemble Japanese
gardens with their pools, bubbling springs, and miniature waterfalls.

While closed to fishing and hunting, the springs support a
thriving population of rainbow and cutthroat trout and other
aquatic life, as well as a multitude of animals, four-legged reptiles,
and resident and migratory birds. Excellent trails and boardwalks
make strolling along the terraces easy for people of all ages. The
U.S. Forest Service has won a national award for the design and
construction of the trails, boardwalks, and footbridges at the
springs. Some of the wooden sections were flown in by helicopter.

Indians camped by the springs long before white men arrived
on the scene early in the 1850s to build roads. A sawmill operated
by the springs for a time, cutting timber harvested from the hill-
sides, and both sheep and cattle grazed—and overgrazed—the area
until the Forest Service curtailed the practice. Old-timers in
Wasatch and Utah counties can recall picnic and camping excur-

sions to the springs, first in horse-drawn wagons and later in Model T Fords, when the primitive roads of the time made such excursions an adventure.

Several graded roads now lead to the springs, entering from Wasatch Mountain State Park on the north, Midway on the east, and via the blacktopped Alpine Loop Summit Road from the west up either American Fork or Provo canyons. Especially in autumn, when oak, maple, and aspen glow on the mountainsides, the loop is one of Utah's most popular scenic drives.

As for the name Wasatch — often spelled Wahsatch in earlier times — it is an Indian name for a low pass over or through the range, probably Weber Canyon, where the Weber River cuts through to the Great Salt Lake near Ogden. This ruggedly beautiful canyon was a frequently used Indian trail that was later used by pioneers before the Donner Party and, afterwards, by the transcontinental railroad that linked both coasts in 1869.

THE HEBER CREEPER STORY

It may surprise many citizens to learn that part of the Heber Creeper Scenic Railroad's rolling stock and much of its right-of-way is actually owned by Wasatch Mountain State Park. The park does not operate the railroad directly but instead has leased it to a concessionaire, the Deer Creek Scenic Railroad Company at Heber City.

The railroad was started in the late 1890s by one of Brigham Young's sons as a local freight and passenger line. Taken over by the Denver and Rio Grande Western Railroad in 1899, its tracks were extended westward through steep and narrow Provo Canyon, where it had to move so slowly around the numerous curves that its average speed over the twisting 25.8 miles was less than ten miles an hour.

Sheep comprised the principal freight. At one time in the early 1930s the depot at Heber City was said to ship more sheep than any other station in the United States. There were stations also at Charleston and places called Wallsburg, Vivian Park, Upper Falls, Nunn's, Caryhurst, and Smoot, according to Rio Grande timetables.

The railroad's pioneer promoters had dreams of extending the line eastward over Wolf Creek Pass (the present route of State

Engine No. 1744 on siding at Vivian Park, on the Deer Creek Scenic Railroad line (the Heber Creeper).

Route 35) to Duchesne, thence along the approximate route of present-day U.S. Highway 40 to Colorado. However, like many other grandiose notions in the boom days of railroading, the extension failed to materialize.

Like many another old-time railroad, its usefulness dwindled with the coming of automobiles, trucks, and modern highways. Its commercial operation ceased in 1968, and some of its tracks were torn up. Three years later, however, a portion of the line was revived by a group of local businessmen and railroad fans as a scenic excursion line running from Heber City to Bridal Veil Falls just east of Orem. Although flooding in the mid-1980s damaged some of the track near the falls, the Creeper still takes a leisurely three and a half hours to make the thirty-mile round trip from

Heber City to Vivian Park, where the locomotive is moved to the other end of the train at a siding. Diesel engines as well as steam locomotives are used to haul a mixture of old-fashioned coaches, lounge and snack-bar cars, with dining cars provided on some special occasions. In summer and fall, the railroad makes several round trips each day, coursing along the Heber Valley, Deer Creek Reservoir, and rugged Provo Canyon.

For further information and current schedules, write to the railroad at P.O. Box 103, Heber City, Utah 84032, or phone (801) 654-3229. Train fare includes admission to the Sons of Utah Pioneers Railroad Museum on the station grounds in Heber City.

A woodcutter's road wanders through an aspen grove.

202

The Aspen Trees—The Singing and the Gold*

One late autumn afternoon, my wife and I were wandering through an enchanting grove of aspen trees just past their golden prime—a time when there are more leaves on the ground than on the trees, when the Rocky Mountain sky is a brilliant blue, and the first snows of winter hover not far over the horizon.

The subalpine atmosphere seemed charged with tension, indefinable but spine-tingling, and the colors, even the deepest shades, appeared almost painfully bright. Suddenly a williwaw whirled down the canyon and through the narrow tree-aisle we were following amid the close-ranked white pillars of the aspens. The miniature whirlwind gathered up enormous loads of fallen leaves and flung them high in the air. Descending in swoops and sweeps, the leaves showered down like thin golden coins the size of little saucers, a treasure beyond the dreams of any Midas.

Like children, we obeyed an impulse to follow the example of the williwaw and ran about throwing armfuls of leaves over our heads. When the grove was calm again, the forest floor was carpeted ankle-deep in dappled gold, green, and copper, with touches of bright red-orange and shades of brown and yellow.

It is hard to imagine a more hospitable scene than a forest of aspens in a high mountain meadow at any season of the year except midwinter. In spring, summer, or early fall, each bright green leaf trembles in the slightest breeze, the ground beneath the trees is turfed with grass and flowers, and clear streams tumble down to beaver ponds that are home to fish and frogs.

Aspens must like humans, because the trees seem to choose the kind of terrain where people can wander through, camp or picnic, hunt, fish, or just contemplate nature. Most people who like the outdoors at all seem to like aspen, too, for shade or beauty or firewood.

Some people like to carve their initials in the smooth white bark of the aspen, along with dates and symbols of love. Although

---

*Adapted from my article in the *New York Times* Sunday Travel Section, September 22, 1968, and used by permission.

to me this is just another variety of the graffiti found on the walls of public places, perhaps the trees don't mind, and they do seem to survive even the most extensive of such attentions.

Bears also like to carve their own kind of signs on aspen trees, where they are wont to mark their territorial boundaries by reaching up as high as they can to scratch the bark. The higher the scratches, the bigger the bear. The next time you notice some fresh claw marks eight or ten feet up on the trunk of an aspen, look over your shoulder. You may be trespassing.

However, it was not the bear but the beaver that first laid claim to aspen as its special property. If it was the beaver — that superlatively industrious rodent — that won the West by attracting fur trappers in the early nineteenth century, it was the aspen that lured the beaver.

Readily cut by the beaver's chisel-like front teeth, the aspen furnishes food from its tender inner bark and dam-building materials from its trunk and limbs, with smaller twigs and mud used to plug up holes. Huge beaver dams, some of them hundreds of yards long, are found throughout the Rocky Mountains. They are often made of nothing but aspen limbs and logs cut into short lengths, about stove-wood size.

When the ponds that form behind the dams fill in with mud, the beavers move on, leaving broad, marshy meadows that soon become aspen groves again, proceeding later to higher endeavors like pine forests. The beaver-aspen combination is one of the best erosion-control measures ever devised by Mother Nature.

For all that its columnar trunks soar heavenward, straight and often unbranching except when bent or broken by snow or wind, the aspen does not aspire to great heights as forest trees go. It seldom rises more than sixty feet, and usually it is about half that. Nor does it live to great age as a rule in the Rocky Mountains.

. But the aspen is an eager tree, and it grows so thickly in its youth that it is sometimes difficult for a man to force his way through the crowd it creates. Yet the aspen is a delicate tree, requiring both sun and water for sustenance, and difficult to grow in urban conditions. Its tendency toward youthful crowding diminishes as the trees grow taller, since only the most vigorous can survive the competition.

I have seen densely packed groves of small aspen, crooked and spindly from overcrowding and no more than six feet high,

although they must have been more than twenty years old; but
such groves are rare. In a mature grove, the trees usually stand
apart as if planted in a city park, providing a nursery for the
seedling pine, spruce, and fir that one day will shade them out.
Aspens never form a climax forest, but are merely an interim in
the scheme of things arboreal.

Early French-Canadian trappers and hunters were superstitious
about aspens, as some primitive people are today. One legend has
it that the cross that Christ carried to Calvary was made of aspen,
and that the tree has been trembling—or quaking—ever since. A
more prosaic explanation of the trembling of aspen leaves is found
in the odd hinge-like arrangement by which each leaf is free to
flutter in any direction, up, down, or sideways, in response to the
tiniest breath of wind. I have often seen one tree in a group of
aspens tremble violently while its neighbors all remained still. (The
tree's Latin name tells the story: it is *Populus tremuloides*.)

Aspen wood has been used for centuries in various ways, a
not-too-surprising fact when you consider that it is one of the most
widely distributed forest trees in the world, found in every climatic
zone except the tropical, even in the mountains of Mexico. In the
United States, the aspen is found from Tennessee to the Canadian
border and from California to Maine.

Technically a hardwood (the wood of an angiospermous tree as
distinguished from that of a conifer), the aspen actually has soft,
spongy white wood, making it a prime source of pulp for paper
and for excelsior and other packing materials. One of its chief uses
is for boxes for packing fresh berries and fruit, since it does not
impart any odor or taste to the produce, nor does it easily stain.

Aspen is used extensively for making furniture and to a lesser
degree for construction lumber. In cattle country, it is popular for
corrals because it is tough, flexible, relatively straight, and does
not splinter. Despite the fact that it rots quickly in damp earth, it
appears as fence posts and rails throughout the West.

Fairly resistant to most insect invasions, the aspen is a sitting
target for tent caterpillars or web worms that can in a single season denude an entire forest. Fortunately, the loathsome larvae
seldom kill the trees. After two or three years of devastation, the
worms eat themselves out of house and home and starve or fall
victim to some indigenous type of virus that wipes out the colony.
Then the aspens undergo the miracle of resurrection and soon put

Bold black and white patterns are left when aspen limbs break off at the trunk.

out tender green leaves again to shimmer in the breeze and turn to gold in the fall.

It is in the Rocky Mountains that the aspens put on their gaudiest show of fall colors. Utah, Colorado, Arizona, and New Mexico are especially favored in this respect. Generally, the flaming gold of the Rocky Mountain aspen tends to fade as one moves north, while in the forests of the northeast the aspens are lost in the riot of color presented by other hardwoods.

The last week of September and the first two weeks of October can be counted on, in most years, to produce a color show of aspens in the Rockies. Chambers of commerce in a score of Rocky Mountain towns sponsor aspen tours, and excursion trains put on extra sections for special trips in the high country. Almost anywhere in aspen country it is hard to get away from the panorama of mile upon mile of flaming gold painting the mountainsides with lavish strokes.

Outlet to the Great Salt Lake from Willard Bay Reservoir.

208

Willard Bay State Park

North Marina

Open all year
Camping, 77 units
Group camping
Picnicing
Group pavilion
Drinking water

Modern restrooms, wheelchair
  accessible
Showers
Sewage disposal
Boating/fishing
Swimming

South Marina

Open all year
Camping, 40 units
Picnicing
Drinking water

Modern restrooms
Boating/fishing
Swimming
Concessionaire

9,000 surface-acre lake; boating; sailing, camping; year-round fishing.

As might be expected for an aquatic park close to Utah's third largest city, Willard Bay State Park registers more than 400,000 human visitors annually, a number exceeded only by its surprisingly diverse wildlife population.

Situated just off Interstate 15 between Ogden and Brigham City, Willard Bay adjoins the great Bear River National Migratory Bird Refuge and thus attracts a substantial share of the refuge's vast numbers of birds, as well as providing homes for many resident animals. The high water of the mid-1980s, however, destroyed or damaged much of the complex system of dikes, ditches, and marsh that gave haven to the refuge's birds. Repairs are planned for whenever the waters recede and financing permits.

The state park, established in 1966, occupies 2,673 acres of land on the shore of Willard Bay Reservoir, a shallow, 9,900-acre bay of the Great Salt Lake. A dike keeps salt water out; the bay is replenished by the Ogden and Weber rivers, by a canal, and by some small creeks.

Situated on land leased from the Bureau of Reclamation, the state park has two marinas with boat launching ramps which are accessible by separate entrances. The north marina is a mile west of Willard City on 3rd Street North; the south marina is four miles south of town and three miles west of Interstate 15. Fishing, water-skiing, and powerboat and sailboat racing are popular activities.

The lake is stocked with walleyes, catfish, and trout, but there are sixteen different species of fish in the bay. Large carp may often be seen (and heard) splashing and sucking in the shallows. Great numbers of birds may also be observed at almost any time of year. More than 200 species have been recorded, including such frequent visitors as white pelicans, great blue herons, snowy egrets, California gulls (the Utah state bird), western grebes, black-necked stilts, avocets, killdeer, and many varieties of ducks and geese.

Less obvious than the presence of wildlife is the fact that Willard Bay's water-supply system is both unique and complicated. Willard Bay is only a tenth the size of Bear Lake, and the two bodies of water are situated fifty-odd miles apart on opposite sides of the Wasatch Range, yet they have a lot in common, including some of their water (*see* Bear Lake State Park).

The flow and outflow of both are controlled and are subject to reversal on demand. Their primary sources, 12,000 feet up on the edge of the High Uintas Wilderness, begin only a mile or so apart as the Weber and Bear rivers. The two rivers meet again in Bear River Bay south of the bird refuge. In fact, Willard Bay is the eastern end of Bear River Bay. But for all their similarities, there is a vast difference between Willard Bay and Bear Lake besides size and location.

Bear Lake is thousands of years old and still is largely natural despite man's engineering. Willard Bay is only a little more than twenty years old and is entirely man-made, a freshwater pond on the edge of the Great Salt Lake. A part of the U.S. Bureau of Reclamation's billion-dollar Weber Basin Project, the lake is formed by a dam twenty-nine feet high, twenty-five feet wide, and fourteen miles long, resting on a rock pad six feet thick on the lake bottom. A perimeter road runs along the top of the dam and is open to public travel on occasion.

Building the dam took six years from 1958 to 1964 and required more than fifteen billion cubic feet of earth and rock. It is named the Arthur V. Watkins Dam in honor of a former United States senator from Utah (1947-59) who was a lifelong advocate of water conservation, including the Weber Basin Project.

Born in Midway, Utah, in 1886, Watkins won a law degree at Columbia University. His varied career included service as a Mormon missionary, lawyer, newspaper editor, farmer, and judge. In 1946 he was elected to the U.S. Senate, where he achieved international fame as chairman of the "Select Committee to Study Censure Charges Against Senator Joseph McCarthy" in 1954. Watkins describes that turbulent chapter in American history in his book *Enough Rope*, published by Prentice-Hall in 1969 when he was eighty-three years old.

Willard Bay, Willard Peak overlooking the townsite, and the state park all take their name from the town of Willard, which was called Willow Creek when it was established in 1851. Later the town was renamed to honor Willard Richards, an apostle of the Mormon church. Born in England in 1804, Richards gave up a medical practice when he was thirty-one years old to join the church in Ohio. He was a member of the advance guard of Mormons that accompanied Brigham Young to the Great Salt Lake Valley in 1847. He died in 1854 from the effects of palsy.

Because of constant concern over possible attacks by Indians, the townsite of Willard was protected by one of the largest forts of any Utah village. The massive stone walls were twelve feet high and two feet thick at the top and enclosed an area half a mile long and a quarter of a mile wide. When the fort proved to be unnecessary, it was disassembled in the 1880s and the materials were used for building homes and in the foundations of the local Mormon meeting house.

A young photographer and her brother on the shore of Yuba Lake.

Yuba State Park

Yuba

Open all year
Camping, 20 units
Group camping
Picnicing
Group pavilion
Drinking water

Modern restrooms, wheelchair
  accessible
Showers
Sewage disposal
Boating/fishing
Off-highway vehicles, nearby
Swimming

Yuba-Painted Rocks

Open all year
Camping
Picnicing
Vault toilets

Boating/fishing
Off-highway vehicles, nearby
Swimming

Warm water, sandy beaches; boating; swimming; water-skiing; year-round fishing.

Utah has nearly fifty state parks and almost as many sources for their names. Most recall persons and places and historical events, but one park claims that its name derives from a nearly forgotten and entirely local song. The song's title was "U.B. Dam," its spelling later altered by local usage to Yuba Dam.

Near the geographical center of the state, Yuba State Park is situated on Sevier Bridge Reservoir, also known as Yuba Lake, on the Sevier River between Interstate 15 and State Route 28. The park proper occupies two areas on the long reservoir — twenty-eight acres at the main campground and marina at the north end near the dam, and 400 acres at the Painted Rocks site on the east shore off Route 28.

At the north end of the reservoir a paved access road off Interstate 15 leads to twenty developed campsites with planted trees providing some shade and a sand beach and wading pool nearby. The southeastern site, known as Painted Rocks for an adjacent cluster of prehistoric petroglyphs and pictographs, has vault toilets, a mile of beach, a paved parking area, docks, launch ramp, but no running water or picnic facilities. Both sites are used for year-round fishing for perch, walleye, catfish, and northern pike (a twenty-one pounder was caught in 1987). The park also serves as a base for fall waterfowl hunting. In summer and fall the water is usually warm enough for swimming and water-skiing.

It is the dam, rather than the lake itself, that has given its name to the park. Ninety-three feet high and 1,275 feet long at the crest, the dam was built almost entirely by local hand labor between 1903 and 1907 as an irrigation project. It was enlarged to its present size in 1916. When the reservoir is full, it extends as much as twenty miles up the Sevier River, backing up 236,145 acre feet of water with a surface area of more than 10,000 acres. Yuba Lake is the largest of several Sevier River impoundments whose total storage capacity exceeds 530,000 acre feet of water, providing irrigation water for more than 400,000 acres of farmland in Garfield, Piute, Sevier, and south Millard counties.

Now back to the name Yuba. Californians would be confused at finding Yuba Lake in Utah, since a city, a county, a river, and a mountain pass north of Sacramento all bear that name. Yuba there is an approximation of an old Maidu Indian name for their village at the junction of the Sacramento and Yuba rivers, meaning something like "the place where two big waters meet." Yuba in Utah, however, is a bowdlerized version of the title of a song, "U.B. Dam," locally popular during the dam's construction. The song proclaimed that the workers were damned if they worked and damned if they didn't because they were paid in stock in the Deseret Irrigation Company, which had the construction contract.

If the men worked, they received stock on which they had to pay an assessment of five dollars a share by doing additional work. If they refused to work or were unable to, they lost not only the stock they had earned but also the assessments they had paid. History provides no explanation of how the men were persuaded to enter such a lopsided agreement, but they all were farmers and needed the dam more than they needed the cash.

Unknowingly, the farmers picked a period of unusually dry weather to start the dam in October 1903. Nearly every able-bodied man and boy in the surrounding communities worked on the dam at one time or another (*see* Otter Creek State Park). By the spring of 1907, the dam had risen to a height of about thirty feet, but melting snow in the adjacent mountains was pouring

Yuba Lake.

water into the reservoir faster than the spillway could release it. The flow peaked in mid-June. Mormon Apostle Francis M. Lyman was addressing a large church assembly in the town of Deseret, forty-odd miles to the west, when a rider rushed in shouting that the dam was in danger. Apostle Lyman promptly adjourned the meeting and urged all present to hasten to the damsite. They did so, and managed to save the dam by some heroic measures, including the blasting of a temporary new spillway around one end of the dam.

Considerable fun was had in the region over the punning name of the dam. The song is one of many turn-of-the-century songs that focus on confusing names of places, like "To Morrow," a song about a traveler who wants to go to the town of Morrow today. One verse of the "U.B. Dam" song (though a line is apparently missing) goes:

> Out west they have some funny towns and funny names as well.
> Now there's a town called U.B. Dam, 10 miles from where I dwell.
> I rode with a conductor once, who was a substitute.
> "Where do you want to go?" says he. "U.B. Dam," says I.
> "I'll not," says he, and grabbing me to choke he did try.
> Jab in the jaw, punches galore, he surely made things hum.
> For when I got to U.B. Dam, I was both deaf and dumb.
> (From the book *History of Sevier Bridge Reservoir*, by Dudley Crafts.)

Readings

GENERAL WORKS

Dean May. *Utah: A People's History*. Salt Lake City: University of Utah Press, 1987.
Helen Z. Papanikolas, ed. *The Peoples of Utah*. Salt Lake City: Utah State Historical Society, 1976.
Charles S. Peterson. *Utah: A Bicentennial History*. New York: Norton, 1977.
Ward J. Roylance. *Utah: A Guide to the State*. Salt Lake City: Utah, Guide to the State Foundation, 1982.
Wallace Stegner. *Mormon Country* (1942). Lincoln: University of Nebraska Press, 1981.

INTRODUCTION

Daughters of the Utah Pioneers. *100 Years of History of Millard County*. Salt Lake City: 1951.
Jesse D. Jennings. *Prehistory of Utah and the Eastern Great Basin*. Salt Lake City: University of Utah Press Anthropological Papers, no. 98, 1978.

ANASAZI STATE PARK

Richard J. Ambler. *The Anasazi*. Flagstaff, Ariz.: Museum of Northern Arizona, 1977.
Michael S. Berry. *Time, Space, and Transition in Anasazi Prehistory*. Salt Lake City: University of Utah Press, 1982.
Linda S. Cordell. *Prehistory of the Southwest*. Orlando, Fla.: Academic Press, 1984.
Clarence Dutton. *Report on the Geology of the High Plateaus of Utah*. 1880.

ANTELOPE ISLAND STATE PARK

Brigham D. Madsen, ed. *Exploring the Great Salt Lake: The Stansbury Expedition of 1849-50*. Salt Lake City: University of Utah Press, 1989.

Dale L. Morgan. *The Great Salt Lake* (1947). Lincoln: University of Nebraska Press, 1986.

Allan Nevins. *Fremont, Pathmarker of the New West* (1939). New York: Ungar, 1961.

Howard Stansbury. *Exploration and Survey of the Valley of the Great Salt Lake of Utah.* Washington, D.C.: Smithsonian Institution Press, 1988.

BEAR LAKE STATE PARK

J. Cecil Alter. *Jim Bridger.* Norman: University of Oklahoma Press, 1962.

Fred R. Gowans. *Rocky Mountain Rendezvous* (1976). Salt Lake City: Peregrine Smith Books, 1985.

Dale L. Morgan. *Jedediah Smith and the Opening of the West.* Indianapolis: Bobbs-Merril, 1953.

Joel E. Ricks and Everett L. Cooley, eds. *The History of a Valley: Cache Valley, Utah-Idaho.* Logan: Cache Valley Centennial Commission, 1956.

BIG SAND STATE PARK

Fred A. Conetah. *A History of the Northern Ute People.* Uintah-Ouray Ute Tribe, 1982.

June Lyman and Norma Denver, comp. *Ute People: An Historical Study.* Salt Lake City: Uintah School District and the Western History Center, University of Utah, 1969.

CAMP FLOYD-STAGECOACH INN STATE PARK

Norman F. Furniss. *The Mormon Conflict, 1850-1859.* New Haven: Yale University Press, 1960.

Harold D. Langley, ed. *To Utah with the Dragoons and Glimpses of Life in Arizona and California, 1858-59.* Salt Lake City: University of Utah Press, 1974.

Charles Kelly. *Salt Desert Trails* (1930). Salt Lake City: Western Epics, 1969.

Fred Reinfeld. *Pony Express* (1966). Lincoln: University of Nebraska Press, 1973.

CORAL PINK SAND DUNES STATE PARK

Mary Austin. *Land of Little Rain*. Cambridge: Riverside Press, 1903.

Donald L. Baars. *Red Rock Country*. Garden City, N.Y.: Doubleday, 1972.

Adonis Findlay Robinson. *History of Kane County*. Salt Lake City: Kane County Daughters of the Utah Pioneers, 1970.

DEAD HORSE POINT STATE PARK

Edward Abbey. *Desert Solitaire*. New York: McGraw-Hill, 1968.

Pearl Baker. *The Wild Bunch at Robbers Roost*. Los Angeles: Westernlore Press, 1965.

———. *Robbers Roost Recollections*. Logan, Utah: Utah State University Press, 1976.

C. Gregory Crampton. *Standing Up Country* (1964). Salt Lake City: Peregrine-Smith, 1983.

Fawn McConkie Tanner. *The Far Country: Regional History of Moab and La Sal, Utah*. Salt Lake City: Olympus, 1976.

DEER CREEK STATE PARK

Leslie S. Raty. *Under Wasatch Skies: A History of Wasatch County*. Salt Lake City: Deseret News Press, 1954.

EAST CANYON STATE PARK

Joseph E. Brown. *The Mormon Trek West*. Garden City, N.Y.: Doubleday, 1980.

LeRoy and Ann W. Hafen. *Handcarts to Zion*. Glendale, Calif.: Arthur H. Clark, 1960.

George Rippey Stewart. *Ordeal by Hunger: The Story of the Donner Party* (1936). Boston: Houghton Mifflin, 1960.

EDGE OF THE CEDARS STATE PARK

Tony Hillerman. *A Thief of Time*. New York: Harper and Row, 1988.

Albert P. Lyman. *The Outlaw of Navaho Mountain*. Salt Lake City: Deseret Book Company, 1963.

Robert S. McPherson. "Paiute Posey and the Last White Uprising," *Utah Historical Quarterly* 53 (1985): 248-67.

Allan Kent Powell, ed. *San Juan County, Utah*. Salt Lake City: Utah State Historical Society, 1983.

ESCALANTE STATE PARK

W. L. Rusho, ed. *Everett Ruess, A Vagabond for Beauty*. Salt Lake City: Peregrine Smith, 1983.
Nethella Griffin Woolsey. *The Escalante Story*. Springville, Utah: 1964.

FORT BUENAVENTURA STATE PARK

Charles Kelly and Maurice L. Howe. *Miles Goodyear: First Citizen of Utah*. Salt Lake City: privately printed, 1937.
Richard C. Roberts and Richard W. Sadler. *Ogden: Junction City*. Northridge, Calif.: Windsor Publications, 1985.

FREMONT INDIAN STATE PARK

See *Anasazi State Park*

GOBLIN VALLEY STATE PARK

Joseph M. Bauman, Jr. *Stone House Lands*. Salt Lake City: University of Utah Press, 1987.
Maxine Newell. *Mi Vida*. Moab, Utah: Newell, 1976.
Raymond W. Taylor and Samuel W. Taylor. *Uranium Fever*. New York: Macmillan, 1970.

GOOSENECKS OF THE SAN JUAN STATE PARK

Albert R. Lyman. *Indians and Outlaws: Settling of the San Juan Frontier*. Salt Lake City: Bookcraft, 1962.
Wallace Stegner. *The Sound of Mountain Water* (1969). Lincoln: University of Nebraska Press, 1985.
Ann Zwinger. *Wind in the Rock*. New York: Harper & Row, 1978.

GREAT SALT LAKE STATE PARK

Nancy D. and John S. McCormick. *Saltair*. Salt Lake City: University of Utah Press, 1985.
David E. Miller. *The Great Salt Lake, Past and Present*. Salt Lake City: 1949.
Dale L. Morgan. *The Great Salt Lake* (1947). Albuquerque: University of New Mexico Press, 1973.

W. Lee Stokes, ed. *The Great Salt Lake*. Salt Lake City: Utah Geological Society, 1966.

GREEN RIVER STATE PARK

Robert G. Athearn. *Rebel of the Rockies: A History of the Denver and Rio Grande Western Railroad*. New Haven: Yale University Press, 1962.

John Wesley Powell. *The Exploration of the Colorado River and Its Canyons* (1895). New York: Dover, 1961.

Wallace Stegner. *Beyond the Hundredth Meridian* (1954). Lincoln: University of Nebraska Press, 1982.

Roy Webb. *If We Had a Boat*. Salt Lake City: University of Utah Press, 1986.

Ann Zwinger. *Run River Run* (1975). Tucson: University of Arizona Press, 1984.

GUNLOCK STATE PARK

Juanita Brooks. *The Mountain Meadows Massacre* (1950). Norman: University of Oklahoma Press, 1962.

HUNTINGTON STATE PARK

Edward Geary. *Goodbye to Poplarhaven*. Salt Lake City: University of Utah Press, 1985.

HYRUM STATE PARK

Bernard De Voto. *Across the Wide Missouri*. Boston: Houghton Mifflin, 1947.

Dale L. Morgan. *The West of William H. Ashley*. Denver: Old West Publishing, 1964.

IRON MISSION STATE PARK

Luella Adams Dalton, comp. *History of the Iron County Mission*. N.p., n.d.

Gustive O. Larson, ed. "Journal of the Iron County Mission, John D. Lee, Clerk," *Utah Historical Quarterly* 20 (1952): 109-34, 253-82, 353-83.

JORDAN RIVER STATE PARK

Thomas G. Alexander and James B. Allen. *Mormons and Gentiles.* Boulder, Colo.: Pruett, 1984.

John S. McCormick. *Salt Lake City: The Gathering Place.* Salt Lake City: Utah State Historical Society, 1980.

KODACHROME BASIN STATE PARK

C. Gregory Crampton. *Ghosts of Glen Canyon.* St. George, Utah: Publishers Place, 1986.

Philip Hyde. *A Glen Canyon Portfolio.* Flagstaff, Ariz.: Northland Press, 1979.

Stephen Trimble and DeWitt Jones. *Canyon Country.* Portland, Ore.: Graphic Arts Center Publishing Co., 1986.

LARK DUNES

Leonard J. Arrington and Gary B. Hansen. *The Richest Hole on Earth.* Logan, Utah: Utah State University Press, 1963.

Marion Dunn. *Bingham Canyon.* Salt Lake City: Publisher's Press, 1973.

Utah State Historical Society. "Utah: Treasure House of the Nation," special issue of the *Utah Historical Quarterly* 31 (963).

LOST CREEK STATE PARK

Robert G. Athearn. *Union Pacific Country.* Chicago: Rand McNally, 1971.

Maury Klein. *Union Pacific.* Garden City, N.Y.: Doubleday, 1987.

MILLSITE STATE PARK

Allan Kent Powell, ed. *Emery County.* Salt Lake City: Utah State Historical Society, 1979.

MINERSVILLE STATE PARK

LeRoy R. and Ann W. Hafen. *Old Spanish Trail.* Glendale, Calif.: Arthur H. Clark, 1954.

Aird G. Merkley, ed. *Monuments to Courage: A History of Beaver County* (1948). Beaver, Utah: Beaver Printing Co., 1974.

MONUMENT VALLEY

Garrick A. Bailey and Roberta Glenn Bailey. *A History of the Navajos.* Santa Fe: School of American Research, 1986.

Richard E. Klinck. *Land of Room Enough and Time Enough* (1953). Salt Lake City: Peregrine Smith, 1984.

Terry Tempest Williams. *Pieces of White Shell: A Journey to Navajoland.* Albuquerque: University of New Mexico Press, 1984.

NEWSPAPER ROCK STATE PARK

Kent Frost. *My Canyonlands.* New York: Abelard-Schuman, 1971.

Polly Schaafsma. *The Rock Art of Utah.* Cambridge, Mass.: Peabody Museum, 1971.

"Ranges, Ranchers, and Rawhides, Utah's Cattle Industry," *Utah Historical Quarterly* 32 (Summer 1964).

OTTER CREEK STATE PARK

Stephen Trimble. *Rock Glow, Sky Shine; The Spirit of Capitol Reef.* Torrey, Utah: Capital Reef Natural History Assoc., 1978.

Revo M. Young. "Robert D. Young and the Otter Creek Reservoir," *Utah Historical Quarterly* 53 (1985): 357-66.

PALISADE STATE PARK

C. T. Albert Antrei, ed. *The Other Forty-niners.* Salt Lake City: Western Epics, 1982.

Gary B. Peterson. *Sanpete Scenes.* Eureka, Utah: Basin/Plateau Press, 1987.

PIONEER TRAILS STATE PARK

Joseph E. Brown. *The Mormon Trek West.* Garden City, N.Y.: Doubleday, 1980.

Wallace Stegner. *A Gathering of Zion* (1964). Salt Lake City: Westwater Press, 1981.

QUAIL CREEK STATE PARK

Juanita Brooks. *Quicksand and Cactus*. Salt Lake City: Howe Brothers, 1982.

Andrew Karl Larsen. *"I Was Called to Dixie."* Salt Lake City: Deseret News Press, 1961.

Marietta M. Mariger. *Saga of 3 Towns: Harrisburg, Leeds, Silver Reef*. St. George: n.d.

Angus M. Woodbury. *A History of Southern Utah* (1944). Salt Lake City: Utah State Historical Society, 1950.

RED FLEET STATE PARK

Wallace Stegner. *This Is Dinosaur*. New York: Knopf, 1955.

ROCKPORT STATE PARK

Marie Ross Peterson. *Echoes of Yesterday*. Salt Lake City: Daughters of the Utah Pioneers, 1947.

SCOFIELD STATE PARK

Philip F. Notarianni, ed. *Carbon County*. Salt Lake City: Utah State Historical Society, 1981.

Allan Kent Powell. "Tragedy at Scofield," *Utah Historical Quarterly* 41 (1973).

SNOW CANYON STATE PARK

Juanita Brooks. *Jacob Hamblin* (1980). Salt Lake City: Howe Brothers, 1987.

Hyrum Lorenzo Reid. *Brigham Young's Dixie of the Desert*. Zion National Park: Zion Natural History Assoc., 1964.

STARVATION STATE PARK

Herbert E. Bolton, ed. *Pageant in the Wilderness: The Story of the Escalante Expedition* (1950). Salt Lake City: Utah State Historical Society, 1972.

Mildred Miles Dillman. *Early History of Duchesne County*. Springville, Utah: Springville Publishing Co., 1948.

STEINAKER STATE PARK

G. Ernest Untermann. *Guide to Dinosaur Land and the Unique Unita Country*. Vernal, Utah: 1972.

TERRITORIAL STATEHOUSE STATE PARK

Everett L. Cooley. "Utah's Capitols," *Utah Historical Quarterly* 27 (1959): 259-74.

_____. "Report of an Expedition to Locate Utah's First Capitol," *Utah Historical Quarterly* 23 (1955): 329-38.

Stella M. Day and Sabrina C. Ekins. *100 Years of History of Millard County*. N.p.: Daughters of the Utah Pioneers, 1951.

UTAH FIELD HOUSE OF NATURAL HISTORY STATE PARK

Linda West and Dan Chure. *Dinosaur*. Jensen, Utah: Dinosaur Nature Assoc., 1984.

UTAH LAKE STATE PARK

Works Progress Administration. *Provo: Pioneer Mormon City*. Portland: Bindfords and Mort, 1942.

WASATCH MOUNTAIN STATE PARK

See *Deer Creek State Park*.

WILLARD BAY STATE PARK

Brigham D. Madsen. *Corinne: The Gentile Capital of Utah*. Salt Lake City: Utah State Historical Society, 1980.

"The Last Spike Driven," special issue of the *Utah Historical Quarterly* 37 (1969).

YUBA LAKE STATE PARK

Dudley Crafts. *History of Sevier Bridge Reservoir*. Delta, Utah: DuWil Publishing, 1976.

Alice Ann Paxman McCune. *History of Juab County*. Nephi, Utah: Juab County Company of the Daughters of the Utah Pioneers, 1947.

Index